KAMATA
KAMATA
KAMATA

(catch catch catch)

Bushpal Publishing

Pete Litchfield

ISBN: 978-1-3999-8091-3

Acknowledgements

I've had a wonderful life and a great career, spent almost entirely with animals. This book focuses on two amazing periods in my life when I was travelling around Uganda, Kenya and Sudan to collect wild animals. I was far from academic, but I was very dedicated and always keen to get things right.

Looking back, I feel very lucky, privileged, to have had the career I've had, which was very unusual for someone from my background at that time.

I'd like to thank the people in my life that made it all happen, angels and devils alike.

This book is primarily for my family: my mother, father, my five brothers, my daughter, Rebecca and my grandson, Henry and, of course, not forgetting the long-suffering wives.

I have thrived on all of the strength and love they have always provided as my family.

My thanks to all associated with this book, for those mentioned within it. Terry Chivers, Brian Vidor and Kit Thackeray – thank you for allowing me to print your personal photos. Special thanks to Ann Olivercrona for filling in the blanks, enabling me to complete my story.

Ruth Martin, special thanks for the inspirational guidance throughout my writing of this book. You made it a pleasure.

Chapter 1

I was employed in Woburn Safari Park in Bedfordshire in England, where I cared for a variety of exotic wild animal species. In January 1974, I was lucky enough to be asked to join the capture team in East Africa, and they wanted me out there very quickly. We were to go out to rural Uganda to capture various animal species for transportation to zoos in the UK, Europe and the USA.

It was all a bit of a whirlwind departure, really, with so much to do before I left. My GP was very helpful, vaccinating me against cholera and typhoid, booking me an appointment in Northampton so I could get a yellow fever vaccination, and organising anti-malaria pills for me. I couldn't leave without all of that mandatory and recommended protection.

A work colleague, who was also being sent out of the country, travelled to Peterborough to get passports for us, while I travelled to London to get a Uganda visa from the high commission, and to collect my air ticket.

Then it was time to leave! Well, culture shock! Wow! *Everything* was new. On my first flight, I was jammed into an East African Airways VC10 charter flight alongside mostly Asian people, many of whom had no doubt been expelled from Uganda by Idi Amin, and were now travelling out to Kenya to visit family and friends there.

I was a novice flyer, and I think I was in shock for most of the journey. The airport had been completely chaotic; I was knocked, pushed and all but trampled underfoot, as people jostled for position and seating, and generally tried to confuse the airline staff to get excess baggage through at no extra costs.

The guy sitting next to me seemed to be something of a contortionist; he managed to get his foot up onto his lap, and proceeded to pick hard skin from the bottom of his foot. An incredible (and slightly disgusting) achievement, especially when we were so tightly packed in on the plane.

I was crushed into a window seat, hampered by a parka anorak I'd worn against the atrocious weather conditions in England that night. At take-off, we were battered by strong, gale-force winds – very unnerving for me, so new to flying. I was actually terrified, and gripped the seat with my hands, legs and buttocks, and then, after those few seconds of weightlessness as the plane lifted off, I sank down into my seat again. The journey passed slowly; the bedlam of the airport continued on board, with virtually everyone demanding the attention of the air crew for drinks, and so on.

It took me a long time to settle down, but I was now on my way, going on the trip of a lifetime and heading to countries I had long wanted to see. I had no idea of what to expect when I got there, I just had a romantic vision in my head. I took no food or drink for the whole trip, as I was afraid to spend any money. I'd only been given £25 for my estimated three-month trip (about one week's wages), and I wanted to save my cash.

We flew through the night to Nairobi, with just one fuel stop in Tripoli in Libya. My view from the plane as it got light was of what appeared to be near desert. Then, amid much commotion, we were circling to land. I was so relieved.

As the doors opened and we poured out of the plane in Nairobi, I could feel and smell the heat, with a mixture of smoke or charcoal. As a completely novice traveller, I found myself in Nairobi Airport for the whole day as my flight on to Uganda didn't leave until 7 in the evening. I was also hampered with not only my anorak, but also a huge suitcase as well – I didn't know I could have checked my luggage straight through to Uganda from London. One of my first lessons learnt.

I spent my time in the airport, people-watching. I watched a very disgruntled American couple, obviously having flight problems; the man was despatched several times to the ticketing office, attempting to rectify their problem, changing flights, airlines or whatever, and each time he looked more and more reluctant to return to convey his non-achievements to a very unhappy-looking wife!

I also watched two men, one of whom was a policeman with a gun, greet each other and then hold hands, smile and laugh together, as they swung their arms. It was a very new experience for me, and it made me wonder what I had actually come to.

Eventually, the time came to check in and go through to departures, ready to board the flight to Entebbe. As we sauntered along, the guy next to me started to talk. He was in Kenya on business, he said, and thought he would go down to Uganda simply to say he'd been there. I said, "I'm not a happy flyer; I would only fly if I had to."

"Oh, flying *never* bothers me. I've flown thousands of miles, with never a care," he said.

I kept quiet, steeling myself for the impending flight and trying not to look scared stiff. Thankfully, I would soon be on board and free from my newfound friend and alone with my thoughts. But no, you've guessed it: I had the aisle seat and he had the middle one, next to me. He babbled on and on, and I just stayed with my own thoughts as we taxied out, ready for take-off.

It felt much like my earlier flight, but although this was a smaller DC9 plane, we had much more room. The engines revved and off we went, faster and faster down the runway. Again, I gripped my seat with every part of me, waiting for the plane to lift. I tried to hang onto my stomach as we went skywards, but oh no! My face was slammed into the back of the seat in front of me, and my newfound friend (you know, the confident, blasé flyer with never a care) shouted, "Oh my God! Now he's done it!"

With engines thrown into reverse, it was difficult trying to prise myself from the seat in front of me. Through a window, I could see the little marker posts that lined the runway flashing past, and I feared we would run out of runway. Newspaper headlines were flashing through my mind, yet I was somehow too scared to be afraid. Then, with much juddering of the plane, all seemed under control again and we slowed quite quickly to a stop.

My so-called friend had now regained his composure, and said, "Oh well, no doubt we will be here for the next half hour while things get checked out." (He knew everything, of course.)

We continued to taxi and eventually came to a stop. It was very dark outside from what I could see, with very few lights at all.

"Will we have to get off, do you think?" I asked my neighbour.

"No, we'll just sit while they do checks," he said.

Wrong again – we were about to take off again. The engines started revving, getting louder and louder, and juddering even more as we gathered speed. Not a murmur from the passengers could be heard as we rushed into the darkness. On we travelled, with no-one daring to draw breath until, once again, I found myself slammed into the back of the seat in front of me, watching as the runway marker posts flashed past. I had nothing more to grip with, every muscle in my body, from my buttocks to neck, felt strained and exhausted. Once the plane came under control again, it did taxi back to the terminal for the engineers to make checks.

We all waited on board and, after about 30 minutes, we were again taxiing down to the end of the runway where we just seemed to sit for what felt like an age before the engines roared again. Once more, we waited with bated breath as we travelled faster and faster, with more expectation of abortion than of becoming airborne. But the nose came up, my belly dropped, and slowly we climbed into the air. By the time we had levelled out, and the hostesses were up and starting to serve passengers, we all started to relax a little for the hour-long flight.

This was a much nicer flight; there were no ringing bells and it was extremely quiet compared with the last flight. Well, I started to think, perhaps flying isn't so bad after all.

I spoke too soon! The plane dropped, maybe a thousand feet, I don't know, and I was off my seat with my belt straining tightly at my waist. I held my breath. Women screamed, kids started crying, crockery crashed at the back of the plane as, again and again, we kept dropping. The air hostesses were sprawled in the aisles, clinging to seats, with legs very much akimbo. The public address system babbled indiscernible words, the lights dimmed, and we began to climb quite sharply again. I could see flashes of lightning as the plane banked left and right.

As the air hostesses scrambled to find their seats, we began to climb sharply again. I had no idea what was happening; it seemed like the pilot was trying to avoid a storm by continually climbing and banking. We dropped again and, once more, my friend sitting next to me was struck dumb. After what seemed like an age, the plane levelled out and the air hostesses resumed their normal duties such as they could, complete with scrapes and grazed arms and legs, and signs of blood coming through stockings. (I knew they were stockings rather than tights, as I'd had a very close-up view of a lot more than stocking tops during our turbulent moments.)

The only thing everyone wanted to do now was to get off this plane. Thankfully, the rest of the journey remained uneventful, even though I kept expecting more scares. When we eventually touched down, I thought, well, I wasn't due to die tonight!

Chapter 2

From the plane, we made our way across the asphalt towards the airport building, where there was a long queue waiting to enter. It was very warm. When I got inside and approached the desk, I could see my boss, Richard Chipperfield, standing to one side. When he saw me, he gesticulated for me to hurry up.

"Come on as quick as you can, we've got a long trip ahead!" he mouthed.

Well, there was little I could do other than wait my turn.

It was quite a relief to see a familiar face and a weight lifted for me, somehow. Richard was our Managing Director back at Woburn Safari Park, and I had spent the odd period of time with him during the building of the park. He was a good boss but he never stopped; he needed to be on the go and achieving *all* the time. Seeing him dashing around even at the airport reinforced that this was not going to be anything like a holiday trip.

"See you outside!" he shouted, and disappeared.

As I expected, he wasn't hanging about.

I got to the immigration desk and a very officious-looking man glared at me, stamped my passport and, with a flick of his head, let me know I should move on. I did, following other passengers to the customs shed (quite aptly named), which was also the baggage collection area. There were piles of baggage and you just had to sort through the suitcases and bags to find your own. Fortunately, I spotted mine quite quickly, grabbed it and shuffled along to another counter.

This one was basically a trestle table, with customs officials standing behind it, checking bags and generally giving everybody quite a grilling. When it was my turn, the young officer smiled at me and asked me how much cash I was carrying. My answer put another smile on his face, even raised something of a chuckle, to say the least. I only had that £25 on me, along with my three-month visa. I guess it must have been quite funny to him, when I think about it now!

I saw the Boss again, heading back out to the immigration area. The customs official stamped a piece of paper, handed it to me and, as he told me I was free to go, the Boss appeared again. I trailed behind him through the terminal, which was more like a barn than an airport terminal, and out to what appeared to be the drop-off circle outside the building. He grabbed my bag and threw it onto the back of a green pick-up.

"Hop in!" he said.

As I climbed in, he said, "Where is that bloody boy now? Chasing a woman, I bet!"

He shouted something out of the window and someone climbed onto the truck, and we zoomed off into the night. Wow! It was a quarter to ten, and we were more than an hour late.

"I dropped my bloody passport when I went to look for you," Richard told me. "Luckily someone had handed it to an immigration officer."

Well, I thought, at least that took the pressure off me while I was going through the customs and immigration formalities.

"You're lucky I came round this way today and got the message that you were arriving. I was in Karamoja and thought I'd come by and see if there was any post and I found the message about your arrival. So it's only by chance that I'm here, but I've been hanging around here all bloody day."

What I would have done if he hadn't been there to meet me doesn't bear thinking about. I had been given no instructions about what to do if that had happened; in truth, no-one sending me out to Uganda would have known what to tell me to do anyway.

I was now at the end of my journey, and at the start of this whole new African adventure. I suddenly realised how tired I felt – it had been some

40 hours since I'd slept and, for the first time, I now felt I could relax a little. I tried to stay awake and stay in the conversation with Richard, but I failed. I would rally every so often to try and be sociable but I just couldn't keep my eyes open. I was aware we'd headed out of Entebbe towards the capital, Kampala, and then we'd begun trekking north.

"This is camel country," I remember hearing the Boss say, and then nothing until he started shouting again. But that was just him chatting with the guy on the back of the truck. I was aware at one point of him reversing a little and then turning sharp left onto a track that was little more than wheel-marks through the grass.

"Almost there," he told me.

Now awake, I watched the track, which seemed to go on forever, and I became quite mesmerised by the long grass in the headlights. Suddenly, I saw little lights coming into view and then we were coming to a stop.

"That's it, Pete, this is home!" Richard told me, as he jumped out of the vehicle and began shouting once more.

I climbed out of the truck and just stood, while Richard babbled on, nothing much of which I understood. I just stood there in shock, really; there was nothing to do but just stand. I knew nothing of where exactly I was, or what to expect. I had no knowledge of the role I would play out there either.

I would have loved to have been able to drop into bed somewhere but I just had to stand and wait. Then, through the shadows, a guy emerged and said, "I had given up on you tonight."

"Pete, this is Charlie," Richard said and, as a female appeared out of the darkness, added, "Well, hello, this is Ann, Pete."

I'd never met Charlie Harris, but I had heard of him, as he was Chief Game Warden at Blair Drummond Safari Park in Scotland. I didn't know anything about Ann Olivecrona at all and, I have to say, I had little interest in finding out anything about anyone at that stage! All I wanted to know was when I could get to bed.

Hellos and introductions all done, the tea was brought round and I grabbed a cup of tea, the first drink I'd had for almost two days. The banter between Richard and the others continued, and everyone seemed happy to stand around drinking tea in virtual darkness, while I just longed for my bed. Nothing that was being said had any meaning for me. When Richard declared it was time for bed, I thought, great. *At last.*

"Pete, me and Charlie are in here," Richard said, pointing to a tent-type building. "You had better go and sleep with Ann."

"Come on," said Ann, and I dutifully followed her into the darkness.

Richard called out, "Up for 5am, Pete!"

I had had literally no idea of what sleeping quarters to expect – life was a complete mystery for me at that point. Ann could have directed me to a hole in the ground, and I would have been happy as long as I could lie down and sleep.

There was another tent-type building with a hurricane lamp on it, and I followed Ann as she walked through the entrance into it.

"That's your bed there," she said. I think she wanted to clarify the situation in case I'd thought about taking Richard's words literally.

From the light of the hurricane lamp, I could see there were two camp beds opposite each other, about two feet apart, but other than that the rest of the area was in darkness. While I was trying to work out where to put my case, Ann jumped into her bed and lay there, with her head propped on her arm, ready for a chat. She wanted to know who I was, where I worked and for how long, and I suddenly began to feel very self-conscious, standing no more than two feet from this unknown female and needing to undress for bed.

"What about the lamp?" I asked.

"That stays on," she said.

Bugger! I was extremely tired, so I threw all my inhibitions to the wind, stripped to my underpants, and dropped into bed. Ann carried on talking, goodness knows for how long before she realised I was zonked and out for the count.

It didn't really sink in at the time, but I had arrived in Africa.

Chapter 3

The din! What the hell? I was being dragged kicking and screaming from my dead sleep and I wasn't at all happy. It seemed to go on and on as I slowly surfaced and opened my eyes. Wow! I jerked my head back and I desperately tried to come to terms with where I was and what the hell I was doing there.

As my eyes focussed, I found I was looking at a girl staring back at me from just two feet away. She spoke loudly above the dreadful din outside.

"There's tea there," she said in her strong Wiltshire accent, and nodded towards the ground.

Ann was Swedish and, I later discovered, had gone to work at Longleat Safari Park a couple of years earlier. Her English was very good – in many ways better than mine – but the pronounced Wiltshire accent coming from a Swedish person really amused me.

Oh yes, it all started coming back to me. Ann didn't appear to have moved from last night – she was still lying in bed, with her head on her hand, and she was still staring at me. I reached down to the floor, picked up my cup of tea and took a sip.

Wow, that was good! Apart from the tea I had when we'd arrived the night before, this was the only liquid to pass my lips since the cuppa I'd had before leaving home in England, which now seemed like *days* ago.

"I think you're going catching this morning," Ann shouted, and nodded towards the door.

I looked out as the Boss looked in. He was sitting on top of a big truck.

"Oh good," he said, when he saw me awake. "Are you coming catching

10

this morning are you going to lie in bed all bloody day?"

Well, that was me up! I leapt out of bed to great cheers from the truck. I looked up and saw the truck was carrying a number of African guys and they were all shouting something in my direction, which was clearly amusing the Boss. I grabbed my case, a large black holdall, threw it on the bed and started rummaging through it. Well, I'd packed it quite nicely but obviously with all the wrong gear, it would seem.

"What the hell am I going to wear?" I said.

"Shorts, if you have them," came the reply from the bed opposite me.

"Well I don't", I said. (As far as I was concerned, shorts were only for holidays.)

My white cord-type trousers seemed like a good option, so I dragged them from my bag. They had started life as a fawn colour but had faded with age. I tried to climb into them as quickly as I could, knowing the Boss was waiting for me, but instead I wobbled and fell onto the bed! I managed to yank them up and, with a deep breath, fastened them at the waist. I grabbed the shirt from the day before, wriggled my feet into the shoes I'd flown in, and I ran towards the door.

As I left the tent, there were more cheers and then at least two pairs of helping hands dragged me up onto the Humber truck and we were off.

Richard was perched on the roof of the truck, and Charlie was in the driver's seat.

"Did you sleep?" Richard asked me.

"Yes," I said, "and I am still sleeping."

Then one of the guys in the back said something to me in Swahili, and Richard interpreted: "He asked how you are."

"Thanks," I said, "tell him I'm a bit stunned and confused."

Richard told him. I'd heard Richard speak Swahili once before, when he was showing some visitors around the park at home. I liked the sound of the language, it sounded nice to speak and I hoped I'd get to grips with it at some stage too.

"Make sure you hang on, Pete, it gets bloody rough at times when we start to catch. Come up front, it's much safer," Richard said.

I'm not sure why, but I didn't go up front when Richard said I should. As a young man, I think I felt somewhat embarrassed by the fuss. It was silly, really, but you live and learn.

We rattled through a river bed, and that really woke me up! I looked back and could see a vehicle with boxes on it following behind us. It was a Bedford TK lorry – a reminder of home, that's for sure.

I was slowly becoming aware of where I was, and realising how very different it was from home. Africa had a warm, earthy smell and, even though it was still early in the morning, the sun was really beginning to warm my body through.

Capturing elephants was the aim of this foray into the African bush, and it seemed to me we had the whole of Africa to cruise through. It was a vast area, seeming to stretch for miles, as indeed it did.

I saw a reedbuck scampering away from us and, a little later, a few Ugandan kob grazing and staring up at us as we passed. Well, this was a very pleasant experience and it felt quite surreal to be there. We motored on, enjoying great views too; in the truck, we were quite high up from the ground and we could see above the long grass and many of the smaller acacia trees and bushes.

It was all so new to me; as with everything else, I had little idea of what to expect on this trip. All I could do was watch and wait.

After a while, we stopped and Richard took out his binoculars to scan the area before we moved on again. Then, great excitement! There was much pointing and chatter from the guys, so we stopped and Richard again scanned the horizon.

"Yes, get on, Charlie!" he shouted down the turret, and soon we were on the move again.

The Humber truck we were in was an ex-Ministry of Defence (MOD) communications truck. These trucks normally had high sides, but this one had been cut down to make it into a pick-up. We'd had one just like it at Woburn for a while. Above both driver and passenger seats, there's a round hole (turret) with a lid that you operate from inside by undoing the fastener and throwing the lid open. This enabled Richard (up top) and Charlie (down below) to speak directly to each other. Also, if you're down below and you stand up, the top half of your body comes through the hole. Richard would often travel standing on the seat with his top half sticking out the top.

Richard leant over the front again, directing Charlie with hand gestures, and we took to the bush. That's when it really did start to get bumpy.

"Pete, you should come up front now," said Richard.

"It's okay, I'll be fine," I insisted.

"It gets really rough and not easy to hold on," he said.

"I'll be fine," I said.

"Well, if you're sure you're okay..."

I said I was.

"If I tell you to get down, get down, or I can't shoot the elephant if it tries to take you off the back."

Looking back on it now, I really had no idea how difficult my first elephant catch was going to be. I was a strong boy, so surely I'd manage a few bumps easily enough? In truth, I had no bloody idea at all! Again, doing the British thing and trying to avoid any fuss.

Elephant were now very much in view and we were approaching them fast. Wow, how amazing was this to be travelling with a herd of elephants! The guys were now holding a bamboo pole with a rope attached, and a large noose. Richard was holding a gun in his left hand and still directing Charlie with his right.

The herd of probably sixty or seventy animals was on the move and the dust was becoming thicker and thicker around us. A large cow elephant stopped and turned towards us, her trunk tucked under and her ears fully out, and the boys all shouted and banged the side of the truck to frighten her away. Thankfully, this worked and she headed off in the other direction.

We continued to pursue the herd, and there was much chatter and pointing as Richard and the guys selected which youngster to catch. The likely candidate needed to be of a size and age to be weaned from its mother, so it needed to have had a good start in life, and be eating solid food. It also needed to be the sex we required.

We would usually capture young elephant at about four years old; the gestation period of elephants is twenty-two months and, as a rule of thumb, calves will wean at two years (taking milk for the same length of time as the gestation period). So, by the time they are four years old, the young elephant are well established. We would keep the sex ratio at around one male to every five females we captured.

At Richard's instruction, Charlie accelerated but then he rode straight over a huge anthill, which flipped my feet high into the air, and I found myself only just hanging onto the truck's side-rail. Two more times, we bounced and rose, my feet flying higher with each bounce; it was impossible for me to control my body at all! I was convinced I was going to go right over the top and was picturing myself with my back against the side of the truck being dragged through the bush. Scary or what? My God, I hope I can hold on, I remember thinking. It sounds a bit dramatic now, but my every thought was about hanging on and surviving this ordeal – and it was all of my own stupid making.

We came to a stop and the guys were off the truck to capture the young elephant; I was crouched down, totally exhausted from the ride. Richard glanced round.

"Are you okay?" he said.

"Yes, quite a ride! Sure does make your joints ache," I said. Talk about an understatement.

Richard climbed down and joined the guys who, by now, had already grappled with the young elephant and wrestled it to the ground. Charlie appeared through his turret and sat on the roof and I went to the front of the truck to join him.

Richard asked me if I could see the box-wagon coming and I looked back.

"Yes," I said.

"Well, wave at them to hurry up!" Richard yelled.

I started waving frantically at them.

"You don't join in with the grappling, then?" I asked Charlie.

"No. To be honest, if you try to join in, you just get in the way. The guys are best left to it. So, what do you think about your first catch?" he asked me.

"Oh, wow, it was exhilarating!" I said.

I didn't dare tell him I'd missed the whole bloody thing! I'd literally just been hanging on for dear life, hoping not to fly out of the truck, whilst performing a routine any gymnast would have been proud of, and I'd seen nothing of the catch. Thinking about it now, "idiotic" is the word that comes to mind for my actions that morning.

The box-wagon arrived and the guys quickly got a box down from the back and dragged it over to the elephant. They passed the capture rope through the box, which three guys were standing on, and the others helped the little elephant to stand up. Then, all in one motion and with quite some shouting and a lot of skill, they slipped the little guy into the box and secured the box.

Smiles on the guys' faces showed their obvious relief. The lorry was now brought alongside the box, with wheels and tyres appearing from seemingly nowhere. The guys began an intricate system of lifting one end of the crate at a time, and sliding wheels under it. They gradually raised the box higher and higher and when it was all but level with the flat body of the truck, they slid it on and secured it with rope. By this stage, there was a risk that the young elephant could overheat, so the guys trickled water over it to cool it down.

"Okay, here we go again!" said Richard, and we were on the move in search of our second capture.

It was slow going at first and then it picked up once we spotted the elephant herd again. The Humber truck was an incredible machine; it was capable of riding over the roughest of terrains as smoothly as a boat on water. (If you're hanging on tightly enough, of course!) I've since learnt that you know it's a good truck when it rises and then crashes down the other side, but still keeps on going.

Having learnt my lesson, this time I was up front, right where the action was and where the decisions were made. I also felt very safe, as all the guys huddled up front, with one actually holding the front rail with a hand on either side of me. At that point, I didn't know any of these guys I was huddled in a heap with but what I did know was that I'd like them on my side in a fight.

I found out later that they were very much a mixed bag of guys – from Kenya, Uganda and the Congo – and they were incredibly powerful and fit. They were an amazing capture team, all masters of their trade, and they operated like a well-oiled machine. They'd leap from the truck and, as one, control the newly-captured animal and secure it from harm. It was quite something to witness.

Obviously, I got to know them all very well later on, and we had a lot in common. We were all young men, enthusiastic and fun-loving. We had huge respect for Richard and we all knew he was the one to please; to achieve that, all we had to do was our jobs.

Again, after a lot of jabber and pointing, we were suddenly in the midst of another herd; there was thick dust, bellowing elephants, a roaring engine and a great deal of shouting and banging from the truck. It was important to keep the elephants moving as we trundled up to them in their wake, and as Richard and the guys selected another candidate for capture.

Once they'd decided, we moved in close to the back of the herd. (I was able to watch the action this time.) Someone handed Richard the catch-pole and he slipped the noose around the young elephant's neck. We slowed down while the rest of the herd continued on its way; we needed to get the little chap boxed and on the lorry quickly before his family realised he was missing.

The guys were ready for action. Much like before, the box-wagon arrived, they took the crate off and slipped the little guy into the box, where it stood quietly. Out came all the wheels and tyres needed to jack the crate up to the appropriate height, while the lorry moved into position. But this time, at the crucial moment, the crate slipped and pinned one of the catchers against the lorry by his head. After much shouting, and incredible strength and energy, the guys managed to regain control of the crate but as they moved it forward, the lorry went back and the guy was spinning like a top, with skin being stripped from around his head as he spun.

I remember thinking if his head were a tree, it would have been ring-barked and the top bit would die and fall off. But he just shook his head, rubbed the top of it and carried on. I have no idea how his head wasn't crushed, because it looked to me like that was the only likely outcome. I soon learnt that the only treatment necessary for most injuries in the bush was a squirt of violet antiseptic spray, which the team always carried to treat animals' bumps and grazes.

It was somewhat horrific to watch that happen, but I reckon I could have coped even if Martians had landed in front of us that morning. My arrival in Africa, the trauma of my journey out, and the general culture shock of the past day had somehow attuned my body and mind to cope, come what may. I think adrenaline had been coursing through my body from the minute I leapt out of my bed that morning.

"Okay, we'll leave it at that for today," said Richard, and it was all aboard and back towards camp.

I didn't even know which way was up, let alone where camp was from here. Thank goodness Charlie did!

The trip back was quiet. It seemed we were all appreciating the surroundings and enjoying the moment. Richard told me about the area we were in – it was very close to a National Park – and he told me a few things to be aware of when you're travelling in the bush. For example, if the terrain changes in any way, slow down and, as they say in Uganda, *wa chunga* (be careful). He said if you came across a dead elephant with the biggest tusks in the world, be sure to give it a wide berth, as it could have died from anthrax.

Now that my first capture was over, I was very happy to soak it all in and begin to inhale my surroundings. Africa really is a wondrous place and I was realising what a lucky guy I was to have this opportunity. That sun! I love the sun and there is always plenty of it in Africa. I took my shirt off to air my bones a little. I found it all quite exhilarating, and the thought of being here gave me an incredible high.

We arrived back at camp sooner than I had expected, and I was now seeing it properly for the first time, as I'd only seen it so far in the dark. I noticed there was a large tree with steps built around it, where you could climb to a lookout point; there was a table and benches to one side of the tree; there was a kitchen tent some eight to ten yards away to the left, and then two tent-type buildings set back, where we slept. The whole area was spotless, the grass cut very short like a lawn, with vehicles parked to the right and a number of spare wheels in a heap. And the moment we stepped off the vehicle, we were offered tea. That was extremely welcome indeed!

When the box-wagon arrived, we all wandered down to the *boma* area (animal corrals) for the offloading. There was an off-ramp and the lorry backed down it, making the bed of the lorry level with the ground, so the guys could slide the crates off quite easily and, amazingly, carry the crates to the *bomas* to release the animals. (I told you they were strong.)

Richard then showed me around the area, taking me to where the maize meal was cooked for the young animals (the *uji* kitchen), then to the hay-barn grass store, where grass was delivered and then fed to the elephants throughout the day and night. Then he took me down to the far end, where buffalo were penned, and to a bridge over a waterway, which they had dammed for use as a hippo pool, if needed. It was also good for a bath, he said, as water flowed through it continually.

We wandered back to the kitchen area, where Ann and Charlie were sitting, with more tea. As we sat down, Richard announced that he and

Charlie were going to Karamoja that day, Ann would be going to Nairobi in a couple of days, and Charlie was having to go home to Plymouth after the Karamoja trip. Charlie was the manager of Plymouth Zoo and quarantine station there.

"That will leave you in charge, Pete."

I wasn't sure I was hearing correctly. I'd only just arrived there!

Ann then climbed into a Humber truck and left to get grass for the elephants' feed, Richard and Charlie gathered some of their belongings together and put them in a Toyota and, as they climbed in, Richard said, "See you in a few days, Pete!" and off they drove.

My God, I really was there all alone.

"Well, it's not so bad," I thought.

In fact, it was a great to have time to actually catch up with myself, my thoughts and just chill for a little while.

A few minutes later, someone came to me and I gathered he was saying he'd moved me to Richard's hut. I watched while he transferred my case and the odd bits and pieces I'd left lying around in my scramble to leave that morning. I went and had a look at my new abode and, as the bed looked so inviting, I stretched out and was just dozing a little when I heard a vehicle coming. I got up again quickly. It was Ann returning with grass and, when she dropped the truck off to be unloaded, I walked up to the kitchen area with her.

We sat and chatted for a while and Ann explained that if you wanted *anything*, you just needed to ask Kambanyoka and he would organise it. (I discovered he was the guy who'd moved me to Richard's tent.) She said it might seem strange but it worked better than to try and do things yourself, so whatever you needed, whether it was water to wash, water for brushing your teeth, anything – he would organise it for you. She also told me about the hippo pool at the far end where you could have a bath, which Richard had showed me earlier.

We had eggs and chips for lunch and then Ann said we should go for banana leaves, and so we drove off down a track and into a village. Banana leaves were treats for the elephants – they loved them, in fact, they loved leaves from any fruit tree available – and buying them in the village was good for the local village economy. At the far end of the village, we turned and stopped at each little pile of banana leaves so Ann could climb out and barter for them. I had no idea what exactly was going on but soon we were loading the leaves into the vehicle, and moving on to the next pile. After Ann had got us ten or so piles of leaves, we were off back to camp.

After parking the Toyota next to a barn, Ann said we should have a cup of tea and then head out to fetch the grass-cutters. We took the Humber truck this time and travelled down to the village and beyond. I found the whole scenario fascinating; I was thoroughly intrigued by the new and different world I had entered.

We slowed down on a bridge as Ann pointed out the Nile. Wow, what a sight! I asked Ann if we could stop, so she pulled over to the side and I got out and looked over the bridge. It was fantastic! It was a truly wondrous spot, with hundreds of hippos bobbing around in the fast-running waters, with such a lush green surrounding area. Incredible!

I found everything around me interesting as we motored on again, turning off to the right down a small track, through gardens and small houses with chickens roaming everywhere, then past a small stream before arriving at a spot where there were piles of grass and the guys sitting waiting for us.

There was a great deal of chatter and laughter between Ann and the guys. I could tell by the glances and nodding in my direction that there were questions about me, the stranger, but it seemed to be all in good humour. Then off we went, back to camp, stopping to drop some guys in the village on the way.

We dropped the grass truck by the store and, as we walked up, Ann said it would soon be dark. It got dark very quickly out there and, indeed, lamps were being lit as she spoke.

"There's just enough time to get clean before we eat," Ann said.

We had the hippo pool for a bath but, for me, I would only do that in daylight. The alternative was using a large bowl of water, which I would take out back, strip to my undies, and do my best to get clean by splashing the water around. Not the best, but enough to stop the sheets from getting too black. If necessary, I would get two bowls of water. I'm sure the locals thought I was very strange!

After dinner, Ann and I sat and talked until quite late. We were just about to go to bed when we heard a cracking sound, after which the night watchman arrived to say one of the elephants had escaped. He ran off to alert some of the guys, who quickly rounded the elephant up and got him back into his stall. During the action, one of the guys got a short tusk in his back, just near his shoulder, so as soon as we knew the elephant was properly secure again, we took the guy to the hospital in Gulu, some seventy kilometres away. He was badly bruised, but his shoulder blade was okay, so we drove the hour back to camp.

I managed to get into bed at 3.30am. What a first day, with never a dull moment. I was a little too tired to drift off to sleep immediately, with so many thoughts running through my head. I thought about the guy who'd had his head skinned (I learned his name was Simba, Swahili for lion). He had come and asked Ann for a couple of pills for a headache earlier in the evening, but otherwise he seemed to be okay.

As for me, my joints ached from bouncing around on the back of the truck. I could hear cicadas chafing in the lookout tree and their late-night performance was the perfect soundtrack for me to eventually drift off to sleep.

Chapter 4

The following morning, Kambanyoka woke me up with morning tea in bed. It felt like a real treat to start my day like this. When I got up, I asked Kambanyoka to bring me some water to wash, and he brought me a metal bowl full. I found that quite novel really, even though I only went through the actions of having a wash; it was more of a mime, to be honest.

When I went outside, Kambanyoka came and said, "Porridge?"

There was an inflection in his voice, so I took it as a question and said, "Yes please."

Ann arrived and sat at the table, so I joined her. Kambanyoka brought us our breakfast porridge and, of course, more tea. The porridge was quite thick but with extra milk for us to add as required. This was just like the porridge I had at home, and how I like it – thick porridge with a generous blob of strawberry jam, so I was a happy boy. In general, the food was all good; nicely prepared and nicely presented.

While we were eating, Ann told me, "We need to pick up David Ross from the hospital in Gulu this morning, so if you take the cutters out for grass, I will pick you up from there and take you with me to the hospital, and then I'll drop you back at the truck on the way back. It's important that you know where the hospital is. The boys will show you where to go for grass, and I will follow on."

I knew David, as he and I had both started out together at Woburn Safari Park, where initially he had worked with rhino and I had worked with the big cats. The beauty of safari parks was that over time, we all worked with all the species.

David had contracted hepatitis A and had been having treatment in hospital. We had to fetch him, as he was being discharged and would be heading back to England.

After breakfast, I duly made my way to the truck and several guys climbed onto the back, while a huge guy came and sat in the passenger seat next to me.

"Good morning," he said. "I am Cipriano Obum Otim."

"Good morning," I said. "Pleased to meet you, Cipriano, I'm Pete. Are you going to tell me where to go for the grass?"

"Yes, I will do that," he said.

We got chatting, and I asked him a bit about himself and where he lived. I learnt that he would normally go out with the grass-cutters or, if there were punctures to be mended, he would stay and repair them. He told me he lived in the village with his family.

We set off down the track, and it was another beautiful day. We saw various animals scampering away as we drove past them: Ugandan kob, oribi and a reedbuck. What a wondrous place this is, I remember thinking.

At the end of the track, there were more guys waiting for us and they climbed on the back of the truck. Following Cipriano's directions, I turned left and drove through the village of Karuma and on along the main road. There were a few people wandering along the roadside, and one or two waved and smiled as we passed. Soon we came to the Karuma Bridge, and once again I glimpsed the Nile to my left, stretching away into the far distance.

It was a warm morning, typical of the sunny African climate, and life seemed exceptionally good. I was beginning to see why Winston Churchill called Uganda 'the Pearl of Africa' after his visit there in 1908.

After another mile or so, Cipriano told me to slow down and then to turn right, down a small grass-track, which seemed to wind between various homes. There were banana trees, mango trees and chickens everywhere. This was a whole new world back here, where people actually lived, and it was so different from what you could see from the road.

23

Eventually, after driving alongside a small stream that then widened out, I was told to stop. The guys climbed down from the truck and entered the abundance of long grass that was growing to the right of us. Most of the grass was, in fact, growing in water, I learnt.

I'd been there the day before with Ann, but today I found it all a lot more interesting as I could take a lot more in. Each guy carried a *panga* (large, hatchet-type blade) and they started cutting the long lush grass with their *pangas,* and tying it into bundles. Cipriano told me to turn the truck around, so I did.

I stopped the truck, turned the engine off, and climbed up through the roof turret and sat on top of the truck, enjoying the morning sun. Several children then arrived and, as well as talking to the grass-cutters, they plinked their little music-boxes, which I found most interesting. Occasionally, if one of them spoke to me, I'd just smile and shrug, just to let them know I didn't understand.

The little music-boxes the children were playing are known in Uganda as *kalimba* (handheld, thumb pianos). They are little wooden boxes with keys made out of strips of metal, a bit like a keyboard, and you flick the metal strips with your thumb to produce a note and, depending on the tension, each strip produces a different note or sound.

When Ann got there, I climbed down off the truck and got into her Toyota and we were off on our way to the hospital. We drove back through the *shambas* (small homesteads) to the main road, where we turned right to Gulu, all the while Ann asking me questions, trying to get to know me and to find out something about me. I didn't really contribute much to the conversation other than just answering her questions, but the journey was valuable for me to see – in daylight – how to get to the hospital.

There was so much to take in, all around me; it didn't feel quite real but it was an amazing morning. All around, I could smell that smell, which became the smell of Africa for me; a kind of mix of soil and smoke. The whole experience was quite stunning, and I'm sure with my wide eyes and facial expression, I must have looked like a kid who was opening the

Christmas present of his dreams.

It took us around 45 minutes to get to the hospital in Gulu, which was a huge place. When we went in, Ann announced our arrival and I sat and waited in the foyer while she went off to collect David. There was a strong smell of disinfectant, I remember; not a surgical spirit smell, like you get in hospitals back home, this was definitely disinfectant.

When Ann and David appeared, I greeted David and we departed. It was a very quiet drive back, as I had climbed on to the back of the Toyota to give David more room in the front. I enjoyed the scenery and being alone with my thoughts, whilst taking in all the sights. It was all so new to me and I became fascinated by how people appeared to live, from my view from the back of a truck. However, we were soon turning left down the little track to deliver me back to my truck and the grass-cutters.

When we got there, several of the guys came out and spoke to David and others were just finishing tying the load of grass in place on the back of my truck. We set off back to camp with my companion next to me to guide me.

As we passed through Karuma village again, there were bundles of banana leaves lining the roadside, ready for the day's bartering to begin. Once through the village, we turned right and down the small track, which led to our camp. It was an uneventful journey back to camp, but I found it somehow mentally rewarding, and it gave me a kind of feeling of well-being.

Back at camp, Cipriano directed me to drive down the side of the animal *bomas* until Edimo, who appeared to be the head keeper, told me to stop. I climbed out of the truck, left the guys to offload the grass, and walked back up to the kitchen area. As soon as I sat at the table, tea arrived, which I was very glad of. For sure, the guys in camp know how much the English like their tea!

After a few minutes, Ann and David arrived back too. Ann said when we'd had our tea, she and I should go together for banana leaves so I could see how it all worked. We drove down to the village of Karuma, turned left, went to the far end of the village, turned around and, on our return, stopped at every bundle of banana leaves. The practice of bartering for each bundle involved a lot of laughter and shouting; Ann was fluent in Swahili, so I found it all quite confusing and I had no idea what they were saying.

Sometimes the bartering went on for quite a while and other times they settled quickly. It seemed to me that the selling of banana leaves was very much an activity for the women and, as well as getting money, they really seemed to enjoy the social interaction. It was all a good-humoured affair and everyone was content with the outcome. I was fascinated by the whole process as all the women seemed to have such a good time.

Once we had cleared the roadside, having bought all the leaves available, it was back towards camp, leaving the Toyota in much the same place as I had left the grass truck.

Lunch was ready by now but I asked for water so I could wash my hands before sitting down. It was good old fried spam and chips for lunch. I have to say I was ready for it, along with copious amounts of cool water.

After lunch, Ann said I should go back for the second load of grass and the cutters, so I set off again with my travel companion, back down our little track to the main road. It seemed there was always something to do at the camp, but it wasn't exactly hard work and every trip was a real pleasure, although it was often quite tiring because of the heat.

Later that afternoon, when I returned with the grass and the cutters, I wandered around the campsite, looking at the animals and trying to get my bearings of the camp layout. There were over forty young elephant and fifteen buffalo in the *bomas*. There were some mud houses, where a number of the staff lived with their wives and children, so I wandered through the estate. I found it very interesting and was even invited into some homes.

There was very little in these mud houses, other than bed-rolls and a cooking stove. It was only temporary accommodation for the workers for the duration of the safari, and all of the houses would be burned down prior to our departure. This was a condition of setting up camp on this piece of land.

The grass around the camp was cut very short so that it didn't attract snakes or any other unwanted critters, which could be a nuisance. Camp was really very smart; even the dung lump (muck from the *bomas)* was in a neat and very tidy heap.

Back at the kitchen area, Mguga, the night-watchman, was building his fire for the night with ample wood to see him through. His meal was to be cassava root, which he would cook in the embers of his fire.

I thought I'd try the hippo pool out and take a bath before it got dark and, as there were no objections or comments, I felt it was okay to do so. I took my towel and strolled down through the length of the camp and stopped at the *uji* kitchen, then on past the last *boma* to the small bridge over the stream, and there was the pool in all its splendour.

Even though it was built for hippos, it really was a great bathing pool. The constantly-changing water made it quite hygienic too. It measured some eight by ten yards, so it was possible to get a few strokes in too, and you could get in and out using the rail by the bridge, which was very useful.

As I understood it, the guys would normally go directly to the pool when they finished work, so leaving it till now was the perfect time for me to take a bath. The others would already have frightened away any unwanted critters and nasties too.

I strolled back to the kitchen area with just a towel wrapped around me and my clothes bundled under my arm. The light was now fading fast and, indeed, the odd hurricane lamp had already been lit. David was chatting with a number of guys, and they seemed to be sorry he had to go home.

By the time I was dressed, the table was being laid for dinner, and there was a jug of water so I drank two glassfuls as I felt I needed it. It was important to keep the fluid intake up as you can easily dehydrate in such heat.

I sat at the table and I was soon joined by both Ann and David. We chatted over dinner, with David and I doing a little reminiscing about Woburn, and the early days before David had transferred to Knowsley Safari Park in Liverpool.

After dinner, we sat for a while before David joined the night-watchman at his fire. When several others wandered over and joined them, it felt like that was my cue to say good night and drift off to bed.

Home in Karuma

Elephant Ugi. Free in Camp

Ann Olivercrona with Vervet monkey

Elephant capture, photo by Kit Thackeray

Elephants at Karuma, photo by Kit Thackeray

Edimo Boma Guy, Cipriano Obum Otim, Tenga

16 foot Python killed after attacking a grass cutter

Richard Chipperfield,
photo by Kit Thackeray

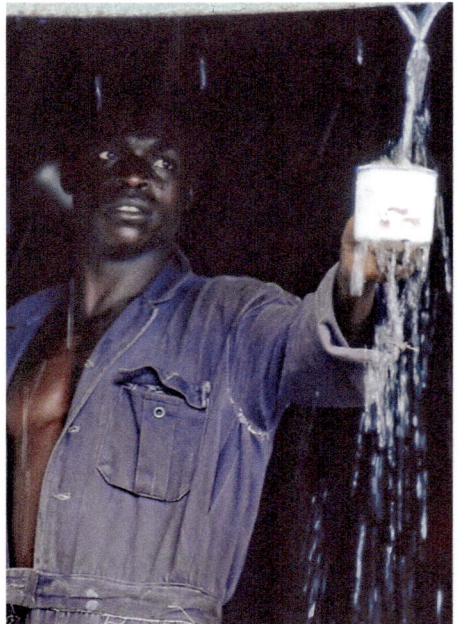

Fishing with Kambanyoka

Johanna. Boy Spanner

Chapter 5

The following day, after my morning tea, I got up and had a wash to get the sleep from my eyes. I went to the table, where Ann joined me, and Kambanyoka brought out a large bowl of porridge for us to help ourselves from. After I had eaten, I went and cleaned my teeth, collected a bottle of water for my trip and, as I was about to leave, David arrived at the table so I quickly said my goodbyes.

"I will see you in a few days," said Ann.

Ann and David were to drive down to Entebbe where they would both catch a flight to Nairobi, and David would then catch a connecting flight back to England. Ann was going to go to the university in Nairobi as she wanted to enrol in a zoological degree course there.

"Right," I said. "I will get on with my morning duties."

Then I asked, "What happens about fuel, Ann?"

"The boys top the vehicles up every morning, and they'll tell you if you need to buy more," she said, before jumping up from her seat.

"Wait! Just a minute," she said as she rushed back to her hut. She came back with money in an envelope, and more jingling in a bag.

"You'll need that! I almost forgot to give it to you," she said.

I hadn't even thought about money...

I drove off down the lane and saw the usual Ugandan kob along the way; I did wonder if I saw different kob each time or if it was always the same two or three. We stopped at the main road to collect more grass-cutters, bringing our team to 16. Their task was to cut enough grass to feed 40-plus elephant for a day.

It was yet another warm day, and Africa felt good – as we travelled through the village and out towards the bridge, the children and some adults would wave at us. The odd woman would wave, point at her pile of banana leaves and hold out her hand, to remind us she had leaves for sale.

When we got to the bridge, the roads were quiet, so I stopped and took a few minutes to climb out of the truck and take in the sights over the water again, which were always spectacular. I peered over the bridge, and the water to my left had quite a flow; I could see the hippo bobbing up and down in the water as I'd seen before, and then I spotted hippos and crocodiles slumbering on the banks. The whole picture was breathtaking – the animals set against a panorama of lush green vegetation and trees close to the river. Looking to the right, I could see the spray of the falls and the powerful, rushing water – it was simply incredible.

However, grass was my mission and the order of the day so I had to get back in the truck and move onward. As we pulled away, Cipriano told me to slow down, and he pointed to the red stains on the bridge.

"The army kill local people and feed them to the crocodiles," he said.

I was speechless.

I drove on and Cipriano told me to turn right off the main road and down that winding little track through the homesteads. As always, the women were tending their plots of pineapples, coffee, bananas and mangos, and the free-roaming chickens were everywhere. Once through the village, we headed out back along the small waterway to the cutting area, where I stopped and the guys all climbed down and headed into the long grass.

I turned the truck around so it was facing the right way and nicely parked, and then climbed through the turret and sat up on the truck roof again. Wow! I just loved it. Watching everything around me: peace and tranquillity in the morning sun, the guys cutting and carrying out bundles of grass, stacking them ready to load onto the truck.

The day before, I had asked Kambanyoka for a pair of scissors so I could cut the legs off my white jeans. I now had a pair of shorts so I could get sun on my legs and, with my shirt off, on my upper torso too. The sun was far from high, as it was still quite early, but it was really warm to the sun-starved bones of this young Englishman.

What a place this was. I also thought about what Cipriano told me. When he came near to the truck, I asked him why the army killed people and fed them to the crocodiles. He hesitated for a while.

"Tribal," he said. "The President doesn't like the Acholi people. This area! Sometimes during the night, you can hear the guns."

(The Acholi people are a Nilotic ethnic group of Luo peoples, found in Magwi County in South Sudan and Northern Uganda.)

It was all very sobering, passing those thoughts and visions through my brain. I wondered how such horrific violence could occur in such an idyllic place.

I went back to looking around me and continued to appreciate my surroundings while the guys cut the grass. When there were enough grass bundles for a truck-load, they loaded them onto the truck and we set off back to camp. This time, it was just me and my now very familiar companion.

I motored along slowly so that I could soak in everything I could see all around me. The women carrying baskets on their heads reminded me of school and my geography lessons, as we'd studied text books that had pictures of women doing just that. Our geography teacher, Miss Wells, had travelled widely with her sister, and had plenty of stories to tell us, which I always found really interesting.

We were soon back on the main road and turning left, heading back to camp. There always seemed to be people walking along the roadside, always someone going somewhere.

I slowed right down again as we crossed the Karuma Bridge – I had come to love these views and sights. I found it heart-warming but at the same time very exciting; it was all so natural but still felt like something of a dream come true for me.

After dropping the truck in the usual unloading spot back at camp,

I headed up for a cuppa at the kitchen area. Everything there was basic but functional; there was a simple wooden table with a bench down each side. The area was slightly raised, which meant we could look out over the whole camp from there, and it was in the shade of the lookout tree – it didn't give much shade, but enough. The lookout tree was large, with steps went around the tree in a spiral up to a platform that you could stand on and, as the name suggests, look out. It was a grand spot, really.

Tea was always ready for us at the camp, no doubt following several years of training by the Boss. I imagine the moment Kambanyoka heard a vehicle arriving, he'd put the kettle on so that he could serve tea as soon as we arrived at the table.

Whist I was drinking my tea, Kambanyoka came to me with the legs I'd cut off from my jeans and asked if he could have them to make clothes for his child. At least that's what I think he said, and of course I said yes – after all, what was I going to do with them?

Cipriano then came to tell me the truck was empty and ready to roll, so I finished my tea quickly and we headed off.

"Wait," said Cipriano. "He wants to know if he can ride to the village with us," he said, pointing to Kambanyoka, who was holding the cut-offs from my jeans. "He wants to visit the *fundi* [expert] for sewing."

"Yes, no problem," I said.

Kambanyoka jumped onto the back of the truck with one of the other guys. This was our now-daily outing to collect banana leaves from the villagers. I'd done this with Ann twice so far, and this was my first such outing on my own.

We drove down the track to the end, where Kambanyoka got off, then I turned left and on up to the end of the village. As we'd done before, I turned the truck around and then slowly cruised along the road until we stopped at the first pile of leaves. Banter started immediately between the guy on the back of the truck and Cipriano.

"Give him fifty cents," he said to me, pointing to the lady with the leaves.

(In Swahili, as in many African languages, 'him' can mean either him or her.)

Okay, I listened to him and coughed up fifty cents. (This was the equivalent of about sixpence, or half a shilling, in old money; about two-and-a-half pence in new money. The East African countries adopted the British shillings but not the pound as their currency, with cents instead of pennies. There were twenty shillings in a British pound.)

I was totally in the hands of these two guys with me, but I thought fifty cents didn't sound like a lot of money. We continued like this and collected quite a load, and I don't remember spending more than a shilling for any single load. The whole process probably took us an hour, with lots of laughing and shouting – mostly directed at me – but always with a smile and twinkles in the eyes. I simply smiled back. Cipriano said the women wanted me to speak with them, so I should learn to speak Swahili. I told him I'd do my best.

On the way back, when we got to our track, Kambanyoka was there waiting for us. Driving back that day, I saw more animals along the track than ever before – this time not just Ugandan kob, but also an oribi, reedbuck and buffalo too.

After I'd parked the truck and sauntered back to the usual tea area, Kambanyoka showed me the little jacket and shorts he'd had made in Karuma. He looked really pleased with himself, and his outing. I smiled and said, "*Mzuri.*" It means 'good', and was one of only two Swahili words I'd learnt so far.

Johanna, the head-man, then arrived at the table and, in the most difficult, broken English I had ever heard, proceeded to tell me all was well. At least I *think* that's what he said. I believe he said the staff were good and all animals were well, and he was very happy.

"*Asante,*" I said. That was the other Swahili word I'd learnt, and it means 'thank you'.

Tea arrived. Great! Well, as you know, we do like tea.

Kambanyoka went back into the kitchen and was starting to prepare our lunch of corned beef and chips. I called out and asked for more tea, and some water to wash, both of which duly arrived. I had a quick wash of my hands and face and then strolled down to the animal *bomas*, cup of tea in hand.

Some guys were putting out banana leaves, which the young eles were dragging in like kids with sweets. These were lovely, rounded, gas-expelling young eles, and they appeared happy and healthy, just as Johanna had said.

The *uji* kitchen was going full tilt, boiling up maize meal for the eles' tea. Edimo, who was head of the *bomas* and keeping staff, then came around the corner, smiled and then (I think) also told me all was well. He pointed at the grass pile said quite a lot, finishing with '*mjani kabisa*', which I took to mean he needed more grass.

I smiled and nodded and continued on my way, thinking Edimo had been reminding me to go and get more grass before the day was out. Yes, got it. I was quite proud of myself, really.

Later, I would realise he was telling me I had brought a big enough load of grass, and not to get any more.

There was a gap of about fifteen yards between the ele *bomas* and the buffalo *bomas*, which was partly a wet area. This meant the animals could wallow a little and cake themselves in mud, which they loved. Then further on past them was the little water course, where the hippo pool was constructed and which, I imagine, was now used by all of us humans.

Ndenaza, Kambanyoka's assistant (the 'Boy Friday'), suddenly appeared next to me and said, "*Chakula tayari!*"

He was motioning eating food, which gave me a good idea of what he meant: 'food is ready'. Ndenaza not only helped in the kitchen but he also made beds, did the washing, cleaned up after us, and carried out any other domestic chores.

"*Asante,*" I said to him. I felt quite proud of myself, and it gave me quite a lift to have used the right word!

Lunch was very welcome, as always, and I drank down copious

amounts of water to be well-hydrated for the afternoon trek back to the grass-cutting area. As soon as I was ready to leave, I went to the truck and started the engine. Within 20 seconds, Cipriano was in the cab next to me.

I moved off slowly, admiring the camp as we went; there were two guys cutting the camp grass to keep it short. They used long-handled slashing tools, which appeared to cut in both directions as they swung them side to side. I found that interesting, and then we were off down the track once again.

Looking at the trees as we drove, I noticed that many of the short-bush trees had an abundance of broad-leafed foliage, as opposed to the much more prolific narrow-leafed acacia thorn bushes. I also noticed that the trunks were all burnt black as if from fire and I asked Cipriano if they had been burnt.

"Yes," he said. "Burned all here. Burned and then grow again."

"Does it just burn or do people burn it?" I asked.

"Sometimes and sometimes," he said.

"Thank you," I said, taking his answer to mean 'both'.

I have since learnt that the trees that had been burnt were some kind of fig tree.

There was a small sentry box at the end of our track, which appeared quite derelict. I'd seen no activity there since I'd been at the camp, but as we approached this time, someone stepped out of it, stood to attention and saluted. In all honesty, his sudden appearance from what had looked to me like a little hovel at the side of the track made me jump. All I could do was glare at him as we passed. I looked at Cipriano, who said, "*Mchezo mlinzi.*"

"Good," I said. "I'll take your word for that."

I later learnt that meant 'game guard'.

We turned left and off through the village. Back in the village of Woburn, where I was brought up, someone once said to me that whenever he drove his car through the grounds of Woburn Abbey, he forced himself to take note of all the deer there. It was home to the largest herd of Pere David deer in the world, and it was, in fact, the place that saved that particular species from extinction, having the only thirteen of its kind in the world at that time. Every Pere David deer in the world today comes from those thirteen animals. He reasoned that it was easy to take such sights for granted, and believed we should always appreciate our surroundings; what we see is just in that moment and never to be seen again.

These thoughts were flowing through my mind as I travelled through Karuma village; I tried to take in everything I saw, as today's picture would be different from tomorrow's, and so on. Tomorrow would be a different time, different people with different bicycles.

I slowed down going over Karuma Bridge, stopped in the middle and jumped out to look over at the wondrous sights yet again. It was full of life, yet soothingly tranquil and naturally comforting. There were bobbing hippos in the fast-running water, various patches of greenery being carried down-river, probably having been ripped from the river banks at the falls by turbulent waters. Magnificent sights!

However, I had to collect the grass and the cutters, who by now would want to return to their families. We continued our journey and, once we were off the main road, we meandered through the little *shambas*. (Cipriano taught me this word for the little homesteads/farms that each family had, where they happily grew fruit and vegetables and reared chickens for eggs and the pot.)

As I'd anticipated, the guys were all awaiting my arrival so I quickly turned the truck around and they loaded the grass and tied it down, shouting new words for me to learn: *tupa kamba* (throw the rope), *fanya haraka* (hurry, do it quickly). When you hear words over and over again, they stick and it is then that you find the meanings, and you're on your way.

Once the truck was loaded, we were on our way again. Life seemed so very good as we sauntered back out through the *shambas,* once more turning left at the main road, then slowing as we crossed the bridge and on up the road to the village. A voice in the back said, "*Simama, kwenye duka.*",

"Stop," said Cipriano, so I did. "This man wants to go to the shop."

Okay, two more Swahili words: *simama* – stop; *duka* – shop. I was picking up quite a vocabulary!

The guy returned to the truck clutching a pack of cigarettes. We continued onward and, just after we turned down our track, I stopped so the village guys could get off the truck, and we continued on to camp.

Back at camp, I sat and drank tea for a while and gazed around the camp, just reflecting on my day. The sun was getting lower in the sky, and I decided I should visit the long-drop toilet. It's basically a large pit that has been dug, then boarded over, leaving a section of board out over which one had to squat to do one's business. It's a very deep pit, a 'long drop', as the name suggests. It was way out back, and it was always an experience going there. I found it difficult not to look down through the little trap-door into the pit below.

Following on from my short toilet safari, I grabbed a towel and soap and headed down to the hippo pool for my evening bath. It was not only cleansing, but it refreshed and invigorated me too.

The little eles were already bedding down for the night, and were basically snoring from both ends of their little rounded bodies! These tiny little vegetation fermentation factories probably produced enough methane between them every day to fuel the *uji* kitchen!

Dinner was ready and Kambanyoka had lit the lamp for the table, which must have meant we were starting a little later than usual. The evening meal was chips, spam and peas.

"*Yama acuna, bwana,*" he said apologetically. "No meat, boss."

Kambanyoka knew quite a number of English words and, when he saw me looking puzzled, which I often did, he would produce the English words for me.

I smiled and nodded, and tucked in. Even the most basic food was appetising and presented well, and I was always ready to eat.

After dinner, I sat with Mguga, as he sat by the fire as usual along with two of the catching guys. I didn't talk, I just sat and listened while they talked and laughed together. I noticed the now familiar sight of Mguga's nightly cassava root, charring nicely in the hot ashes, ready for his evening meal. It seemed all were happy with their lot.

After maybe half an hour, I got up, said good night and departed to my little abode for the night, having taken a quick pee out back. Sleep always came easily once I'd made sure the mosquito net was well tucked in. The mosquitoes' whining little buzz became the norm throughout the night, as did the cicadas' chafing in the tree outside. Later in the night, when all was quiet, a hippo would come and graze next to my hut too. That sound, in itself, was quite soothing and sleep-inducing. Back home, I'm sure there were night noises too but here life was so different, and we were open to the elements of nature.

The African bush was simply wonderful.

Chapter 6

Early the following morning, Johanna came to see me as I lay sipping tea in my bed. Through his very broken English, I think he reminded me that I needed to get the grass-cutters out to cut the grass.

I finished my morning cuppa and rose to meet the new day. A pee first, then I'd ask for water to wash, followed by a quick rake through the hair – morning ablutions done – before heading to the table.

Kambanyoka greeted me with, "*Jambo, bwana. Habari za asubuhi?*" (How are you this morning, boss? Porridge? Toast?)

I told him I was good (*mzuri*), simply responding to him in the usual way. You can get it very wrong making assumptions, but I was sure about the porridge or toast question!

"Toast, please," I said.

Wow, we had bread! I savoured my two pieces of toast as I drank down more tea. That made a really pleasant change from the usual breakfast, and I'd only been here a few days. I then went to the kitchen door, where Ndenaza was having his breakfast. I looked at Kambanyoka and asked, by gesticulating, for water for teeth, and a little can of water duly arrived at the table.

I collected my tooth brush, applied toothpaste, grabbed the water from the table, and set off on my usual little route around the back of my sleeping quarters. As I walked, I was brushing vigorously, then spitting and rinsing, finally washing the brush in the remains of the water before chucking it away. There, ready for the day! I went back and dropped the can on the table, and then headed to the truck.

Everyone was a step ahead of me and on the truck within a minute, and soon we were off down the track. It was all much the same as usual, travelling down the track to the end where we collected more cutters, then on down the main road through the village, over the bridge, and turning off through the *shambas* to deposit the guys to cut the grass.

While they were cutting, I spent my time as before, topping up the good old tan, simply baring the bones to the sunlight and soaking up the whole scenario. Even the young kids put in an appearance again with their music boxes, plinking away on the metal keys.

When the guys were finished, everything was loaded and tied down on the back of the truck, and we were about to leave for home, the engine stopped. I tried time and again to restart it. I'd wait for a reasonable period, in case it had flooded, and try again but no, it didn't sound even close to starting.

"Well," I said, "I will have to go back to get another truck."

My trusty companion, Cipriano, said, "Yes, I go back."

I had to think what he meant, for a second, but when I started to walk, he came and joined me. It was very hot, as we walked along the waterway, then through the *shambas,* where it seemed everyone was out tending their plantations. They stopped and looked quite surprised to see me on foot, but smiled and quite a lot of gabble passed between them, to which I smiled as usual, and kept walking. I was fascinated seeing the exotic fruits growing: bananas, papaya and pineapples, peanuts drying in the sun, coffee, cherries, and cotton. One lady brought me two small bananas (each about two inches long), which I ate as we walked. They were delicious.

Not so much a walk, as an education, I remember thinking.

We must have walked for more than half an hour before we got to the main road, by which time my shirt was soaked with sweat. We carried on walking and, after a while, came to the Karuma Bridge and, of course, I couldn't pass by without stopping to take it all in. It really was incredibly beautiful, and the view from the bridge stunning. I just stood in amazement at the number of hippos; this time there were hundreds, if not thousands of them, spanning the whole Nile and for as far as I could see, which was a hell of a long way. They bobbed up and down, and let out their deep grunting laughter sound, huge mouths open as warnings to others getting too close to their personal space, although to me it didn't seem that they had any. And the banks of the river were littered with huge numbers of crocodiles, just basking in the heat. Incredible!

As we continued our trek, a bus came along and Cipriano flagged it down. The bus was packed but we each managed to get a foot onto the steps and to hang onto a handrail. It was very hot hanging on the outside, but goodness knows what the temperature was like inside the bus.

We eventually arrived in Karuma, and I was relieved to step down from the bus as my calf muscles were starting to go into spasm. Also, it was bloody hot.

We walked a little way, and Cipriano talked to various people and then told me to wait. I did, and a few minutes later, a man appeared with a bicycle.

"Give him money," Cipriano instructed me.

I took ten shillings out of my pocket. He smiled, took it from me, gave the money to the man with the bicycle and gave me the bicycle. I cycled along the road, turning right down our little track, and what a treat it was, cycling in the African bush almost silently – the animals didn't even hear me until the last minute, giving me great sights and views, and them a fright. On reflection, I never really gave any thought to my own safety cycling in the bush. I was simply caught up in the moment.

About three miles further on, I arrived in camp. There was great excitement and laughter at the sight of the *mzungu* (white guy) riding a bicycle!

I relaxed at the table and drank copious amounts of water to rehydrate. Soon after, Cipriano arrived on foot. No doubt he'd been running then walking, as I'd seen the guys do on occasion. Johanna joined us and the two of them chatted about what had transpired.

45

Johanna then said, "We go, I was boy spanner."

Interesting!

They loaded tools into a Toyota Jeep, and I drove the three of us back to the grass-cutting site. When we arrived, Johanna went to work on the truck, while the guys loaded the grass onto the Jeep. Cipriano and I then departed, deposited the grass back in camp and went into Karuma for the banana leaves, returning the very handy and welcome bicycle back to its owner. There was much banter, as usual, during the banana leaves' bartering sessions, no doubt at my expense as the cycling *mzungu*.

The bartering always took time, and once we'd finished shopping for leaves, it was back to camp to drop the leaves off and to replenish my body's water supply. My morning walk and cycle were just starting to catch up with me too.

Soon we were ready to roll again, and we set off on the next grass run. This time, another person climbed onto the Jeep to travel with us. When the Jeep was laden with grass and ready for me to drive back to camp, Cipriano pointed to the new guy who had accompanied us on the way out and told me he would wait for the truck and drive it back.

"He is Kiprono, he drive the lorry. We can go," he said, so we did.

The Bedford truck arrived back just before dark, with Johanna and Kiprono, and was loaded with grass. They parked it by the grass store until the morning. I thanked them both, and asked Kiprono if it had been a big problem with the truck.

"No, is all right," he said.

In truth, his big problem would have been trying to explain the problem to me.

After dinner, which I ate by the light of a hurricane lamp, I watched Mguga prepare and light his fire (even he was late tonight), and some of the other guys went over and sat with him. Some took their plates of food with them and chatted around the fire while they ate. I also wandered over and was invited to sit down. I just listened, and occasionally they would speak to me, but deep down I knew it was a useless exercise, so after a while I got up and went to my little hut and prepared for bed.

A different day: a long walk in the searing heat, a bus ride on just one foot, and a pleasant bicycle ride.

I was *very* tired, but what a great day!

***

Elephants in camp

Being alone in our Karuma camp gave me the feeling of being very close to nature. I was never really totally alone though, as there were always plenty of staff with their families on site. However, when there were no other people around to distract me, I did find I had the chance to use my senses naturally, as I soon came to discover...

As a young man, I would sleep very soundly through the night and had a strong reluctance to leave my bed in the mornings. At home, I always used the age-old trick of leaning from my bed and banging on the bedroom floor so that my mother would think she had succeeded in rousing me from my sleep with her morning call, while I desperately hung on for those extra few minutes of sleep.

But all that changed with my arrival in Africa, especially when I found myself alone and in charge of camp after little more than a day.

Although my nights were very restful, it took very little to rouse me – the slightest unusual sound would bring all my senses to the fore. I'd already come to accept the sound of mosquitoes, of cicadas in the trees, and hippo grazing close by as normal. As awful as it was, even the distant gunfire as local people were being executed by Ugandan soldiers on the Karuma Bridge became a familiar sound.

Other sounds became everyday for me too. I would hear Ndezana sliding through the kitchen's bamboo door-cover to start his day; I would hear his tread as he started walking in my direction from the kitchen with my very welcome morning tea.

Africa is a very special place and, living as we did, we were right in the heart of life in the bush; I learned to live on my wits a little, using my senses and instincts as much as possible. This was a major survival tool for me. Much like other creatures of the bush do instinctively, I was learning to co-exist in the wilds of Africa, the natural world and my new surroundings.

Game animals automatically know the meaning of every noise and every silence, they know which is harmless and which means that danger is close by. Although it's instinctive to them through their heightened senses, they can still be outsmarted by a cunning predator.

Despite their size, elephants move very quietly through the night, and one only suspects danger when other night noises stop, or you hear the sudden flight of an animal close by, scampering away through the undergrowth for no obvious reason. By this time, the elephants are often very close to or are already inside your camp.

When this happens, the next fifteen to twenty minutes are total chaos, and pandemonium reigns. We rush to the vehicles, rev the engines, bang metal bins and oil drums, and even fire rifles and shotguns into the air. Time is of the essence; if you don't remove the elephants from camp quickly, they will break down the animal *bomas* and release all the captured animals, which could amount to the undoing of several months' work. They could also destroy the human habitation too.

We had to rely on our human cunning to protect our camp, so we didn't end up coming second-best, as our ancestors once would have. One way we did this was by maintaining a small sanctuary in which to relax in relative safety.

Africa is not the perfect place that romantics would often have us believe. It is a fantastic natural world, but is far from idyllic. It is a world where a variety of species have to hunt or travel miles every day in search of a meal or, worse still, they could be the next meal. Just how perfect is that?

So picture the scene one night, with this young, sleep-loving *mzungu* left in charge of camp. It's bad enough the sight of a naked young man rushing from his bed in the dead of night, trying to don shorts and desert boots, daunted by the thought that he might have to take to the bush in greater haste, as our ancestors would have done, running for life itself, while the acacia tore at his birthday suit and various other bits and pieces important to man. But also making sure to avoid the other dangers of the night, like dropping into leg-breaking warthog holes, colliding with trees, or anthills, and being vulnerable to other predator attacks, quite apart from evading the rampaging elephant herds to the rear. It's a wild sight!

In Africa, one often experiences short, frantic periods when peace gives way to turmoil and carnage, before peace returns once more.

So too, as in the above scene of chaos and semi-nakedness, once the elephant herd had been successfully turned, and the dust settled, camp returned to being a tranquil sanctuary. You could once again hear the cicadas chafing in the trees and even the hippo returning to graze nearby. The sight of fireflies as they flickered around had something of a tranquillising effect too.

It always takes time for the body to calm down once the adrenaline from the chaos stops pumping, and before the sandman returns, inducing welcome sleep to the tired bones. Tea helps too. Well, I am English.

Chapter 7

The following morning, I was up bright and early and strolled down through the animal *bomas,* where some elephant were up while others still slumbered, as usual expelling gas freely from the previous day's fodder. Amazing that the plump little young eles all seemed totally at ease with their situation.

They would all know by now that the day would start with the *uji,* a porridge made from maize meal, in fact much as the African people would eat it too. It was a versatile food, being made as porridge in the mornings, then much stiffer like mashed potato for dinner. It would be eaten with vegetables, plantain, cabbage or the like, and with meat, if and when it was available. Later, I would have to survive on it too; I had no complaints, as long as it had been cooked long enough, otherwise it could seem a little gritty.

I took the opportunity to splash a little hippo pool water over my head and on my face. The water very soon dries under the African sky but it's cooling while it lasts. The buffalo were mostly still sitting around, as it was still a little early for the staff to be there too. I leaned against the little handrail on the bridge that crossed the pool, and soaked up the ambience and the incredible world around me. The African bush was a really wondrous place, once a dream for me, but now very much a reality.

I went back for breakfast and a real treat: *mayai na toast* (eggs and toast) and more tea, of course. Breakfast was followed by the morning ritual of a visit to the long-drop, wash, brush teeth and ready for off.

The mornings would heat up slowly as the sun was rising, and there was a stillness in the air. It is a great time of day and you would know it would be another scorcher later.

People were gathering around the truck now, so I climbed into the driving seat with my usual passenger joining me immediately.

"Not yet," Cipriano said.

"Okay, no problem," I said.

We could soon feel the movement on the truck as the cutters started climbing aboard.

"Okay, we go," Cipriano shouted, so I started the engine and pulled away, heading to our little track once more.

"Today we cut grass in Karuma," he said.

"We do?" I said.

"Yes."

"Why?"

"There is much grass, and very close for us."

"Sure?"

"Yes, no problem."

So when we joined the main road, my co-pilot told me to turn right, and so I did.

"*Poli poli*," he said, and I knew from his hand gesture he meant 'go slowly'. A few yards on, he said, "*Acha*." (Stop.)

Once the guys had all climbed down from the truck, I drove a little further along the road and turned around to go back to the drop-off spot. It was always a surprise to me that there was so little traffic. The roads were really good, and I learned later that they were among the last things the British financed before they pulled out of Uganda.

I sat for a while before deciding I would explore the village, so I climbed down and strolled on along the road. There were very few people about as I walked along the front of the buildings which lined the road, shaded by large trees. Then I came across a few people sitting around a little table, and they were playing some sort of game – it was a bit like checkers, or draughts, and they used bottle tops for pieces. A little further on, there was a shop (*duka*), so I went in to explore.

There were various coloured signs, displaying Kimbo (a type of lard in a tin), Sportsman cigarettes, and Lifebuoy soap. A lady suddenly appeared in front of me with a large grin and speaking many words I did not understand.

"Hello," I said, to which she replied "*Jambo bwana.*"

I felt very inadequate, almost regretting being so nosy by going into the shop.

"Cigarettes," I said.

"*Sigara*," was the reply, followed by more words I did not understand.

Taking a guess, I said, "Sportsman."

"*Ndio*," she said, and produced a pack of 20 cigarettes, already open.

"*Ngapi?*"

I guessed she was saying 'how many?', and I said, "*Packeti moja,*" (one packet) hoping that the answer was right. (Shops would sell cigarettes individually or by the full pack.)

A full pack arrived, to which she uttered something, and then, "*Shilingi.*"

I offered a five shilling note and was given four back. I was a smoker, but all of our cigarettes were bought by Richard, with box upon box in our camp store. I just felt I needed to make the gesture by buying something. We all smoked Sportsman cigarettes; ours were made in Kenya and, as I quickly found out, were far superior to the Ugandan-made ones. I felt sure the cutters would be glad of them anyway. I took my box of Sportsman, thanked her (*asante*) and left.

Wandering back towards the truck, I saw there was quite a gathering around the truck and, as I approached, heard raised voices which was somewhat disconcerting. I continued, and on arrival attracted Cipriano's attention and asked him what the problem was.

"This man said we are cutting his grass and he wants to be paid for it. He has stopped the work and demanding money, or he will go to the police."

"Okay, is it his grass?"

"No! It doesn't belong to anyone."

"Okay, what do we do?"

"I don't know."

"Well," I said, "if we are sure the grass does not belong to this man, why don't we call the police to come and deal with him?"

"Yes, we will call the police," he said and went back and joined the group by the truck.

Soon after, one man ran off down the road and returned with a gentleman, who immediately entered the fray. After a few minutes, the man who had claimed the land was his wandered off up the road, mumbling to himself and obviously very unhappy. Cipriano came over to me with the other man.

"This is our policeman here in Karuma."

Well, he wasn't in uniform and he didn't look like a policemen to me but all the others accepted that he was, and he had got the job done.

"He has told that man that if he continues to stop our work, he will put him in jail, so he has now gone."

Then Cipriano quietly added, "Give him money."

Oh yes. I pulled some notes from my pocket and Cipriano grabbed ten shillings and gave it to the policeman, who seemed very happy with it. He smiled and waved.

"*Asante sana*," (thank you very much) he said, and departed along the road.

The cutters went straight back to work and were soon bringing out bundles of grass for loading.

On the edge of the village, where we were, life was very pleasant too. I took up my usual position atop the wagon, and watched as several young women passed by carrying their wares. In fact, one or two made for exceptional viewing, but that came to an abrupt stop when I heard the words, "*Twende bwana!*" (We go.)

Off we headed back to camp with the load. Just a few minutes on, two really large buffalo crossed in front of us, and I had to stop for them – they were not going to be rushed, that was for sure! They were two large males and they feared very little. Buffalo are responsible for so many human deaths in Africa, and it made me realise just how vulnerable those young women were, carrying out their morning chores with such belligerent animals so close by.

On then, and down the track back to camp, where we dropped off the grass in the usual spot. Feeling very thirsty, I guzzled plenty of water followed by two cups of tea.

I then had a quick wander around the animal *bomas*. The little eles were always fun, and the guys had one that wandered around camp. He was always trying to get into the *uji* kitchen and getting chased out, and he looked like a naughty schoolboy whenever he looked up and saw you unexpectedly. His mock-charges were comical too, with trunk tucked under and ears spread wide, like Dumbo about to take to the air.

I enjoyed mixing with the *boma* guys too, they were a good gang and always appeared to be happy. That was probably down to Edimo, the head guy of the *boma*. I would often hear laughter while Edimo spoke – it was probably some comical statement at my expense, but they were happy guys and they did a good job, which is what was required.

It was soon time to haggle over banana leaves again, so I headed back to the truck. As we drove through the village, Cipriano said, "Do you see?"

He was pointing at people sitting around a table.

"There is the policeman from this morning. Now he has money, so he is drinking *pombe!*"

Indeed he was. *Pombe* is the Swahili word for alcohol, which can mean beer or spirits. The local village beer always looked like someone had thrown a handful of soil into a glass of water, and the local village spirits, *waragi* (a type of gin), was produced, I think, from bananas. It could be – and quite often was – detrimental to your health.

I was now starting to enjoy the banana leaf-buying experience, especially now that I knew a few more words of the local language. Indeed, it really was good fun interacting with the locals, although I would always look to Cipriano for reassurance before sealing a deal.

We got back to camp and it was close to lunchtime, so I pondered the day's events while waiting to tuck in. Spam and eggs with chips today. Well, a little different but, as always, so nicely presented and prepared.

The afternoon went by much the same as usual, but I set out early to collect the grass so I could go to Karuma Bridge on the way. I stopped and spent time wandering along the bridge, looking over at the river and its inhabitants. I then crossed to the other side of the road and looked up towards the falls. The spray created a kaleidoscopic vision as it rose into the air around it, the rocks and boulders supporting the gushing waters as they spewed and cascaded down from the main falls, settling into a torrential flow to pass under the bridge and then into a steady flow.

Must get on, I thought, as the guys would be wanting to get finished for the day. So I returned to the village, where the guys were just finishing up.

The remainder of the trip seemed to go to plan and I was beginning to exchange the odd word with the guys, which added to the joys of where I was and what I was actually doing. Surreal is an understatement, really.

As we rolled back into camp, the picture immediately appeared different. Another Toyota Land Cruiser was parked, and another tent erected alongside Ann's. I parked the truck and wandered up to collect tea in the usual spot, and Richard appeared from the new tent.

"Well, hello!" he shouted, grinning widely. "How's it all going? You're still alive, I see."

"Great, no problem," I said. "Enjoying my time in paradise."

He laughed.

Ann also appeared and we sat and drank tea together at the table.

"You must have arrived just after I went out for grass," I said. "You've already had another tent put up."

"Yes, we've been here a while," Richard said. "In fact, Ann arrived just a few minutes after me."

After tea and a little banter, we walked around the animal *bomas*, checking animals, with Richard chatting to all the guys as we went. Everyone seemed genuinely pleased to see him and greeted him with smiles. Edimo was very much his usual full-on self, with much to say and lots of laughter and good humour – he was someone Richard had a lot of respect for. We watched the little eles a while too, as they were always entertaining, and we were charged by Uji, the little guy that ran loose in the camp.

"Okay, let's head back," said Richard, "and Pete, the holiday's now over. We catch elephant tomorrow morning, bright and early."

"Right, okay," I said.

We sat back at the table and I asked Ann how her trip had gone. She said it had gone fine, and said she'd have to go back again to finalise everything but she said that could probably wait until the end of the safari.

We chatted for a while, and I kept watching as the guys finished work and took their baths. For some reason, I felt really dirty and very much in need of submerging up to my neck in water. I had probably sweated a little more than usual after wandering along the bridge in the heat of the day, but it had sure been worth it. Those magnificent sights I witnessed at the bridge were awesome, really awesome.

Having cleaned up, we all took dinner together, with Richard saying we also had to get meat the following day.

"This awful tinned stuff is okay, but we need proper meat."

Through dinner, I related my tales of breaking down, walking back to camp, riding a bicycle, riding a bus, and calling a policeman, as it was all so new to me, and unthinkable back home.

Soon after dinner, we all dispersed with a final reminder from Richard: "Bright and early in the morning!"

After a chat between ourselves, then sitting with Mguga and listening to the *mneno* (words) of the day, it was once again time for bed.

Chapter 8

My first day behind the wheel for an elephant catch and, I have to say, I was a little scared. However, Richard knew his business well, he was a good teacher and he went out of his way to instil confidence. The Humber truck all but floated as we travelled out into the bush, with me driving, Richard up front and six catching guys on the back.

This was my very first capture expedition. I was young, enthusiastic, and probably a bit naive, but I had a job to do. We seemed to spot elephant very quickly and I was soon really motoring through the bush. From a distance, you could be forgiven for thinking they were large trees on the horizon but then they moved across the skyline. Richard said he thought there were maybe sixty elephant in the herd, and I kept moving in closer.

I was then instructed to stop. Richard turned, shouting, "*Weka ubao mbele!*" (Put the plank in!)

At this, three guys carried what was a very heavy ironwood board to the front of the truck, slotted it in a position to cover the radiator, then scurried back on board. We had these boards made specially to protect the truck's radiator (and us) from attack. If the matriarch of the herd were to come back at us, she'd really mean business and she'd attack the truck, usually the radiator area. We'd put the board in place just before we went into the herd; any sooner, and the radiator would boil over through lack of air to it.

"Let's go, Pete!"

We left the track and, taking to the bush, zoomed right up to the back of the elephant herd, which by now was on the move. After some deliberation, Richard selected the animal to be caught. A thick, fog-like cloud of dust followed the herd, making visibility really difficult for me as the driver, especially as we moved in closer.

I was now starting to take direction from Richard's hand signals only – a strange sensation for sure. The Humber truck took some driving too – power-steering would have been a great asset once we'd left the track and had to push on through the bush. I also learnt my first valuable lesson of the safari that morning: not to steer the truck with my thumbs tucked around the steering wheel. If you do, when the front wheels hit a rock or any other solid object, or even one of the many anthills dotted around, the impact makes the steering wheel spin, yanking your thumbs back against your wrists. It's excruciatingly painful, as you can imagine, and I learnt this the hard way. It was a bit of a wake-up call, for sure, but it meant I very quickly got the hang of it.

I could see nothing but dust ahead of us, so I had little time to comprehend the large shape of an elephant heading straight for us. She hit the front of the truck with a real juddering bump, then mounted the bonnet and thrust her head through the open windscreen right in front of me. I leant hard to my left and only just managed to avoid her massive tusks, which hit the metal panel just behind me. Thank God I moved; those tusks would have otherwise gone straight into my head.

"Push her, Pete!"

I stepped on the accelerator, the power slowly pushing the elephant into retreat and eventually turning her. I was relieved to see her trundle away from us, but the guys on the back continued to bang on the side of the truck and shout. I kept revving the engine, keeping the pressure on her to move on and catch up with the herd, but she stumbled. She desperately tried to keep her feet but, with the momentum of her three-and-a-half tons of slate-grey skin and bone, her legs buckled and the great beast hit the ground head first and rolled over onto her side. She wasn't hurt – well, maybe her pride was hurt – but she would need time to get up.

Once they go that flat, elephant have to rock back and forth until they're in a position to heave themselves up; it can take several minutes for them to get back up on their feet. Elephant can be extremely dangerous – especially this one as she'd already tried her best to kill me – so we took advantage of this reprieve of time, space and a little safety, to achieve our capture of a youngster from the back of the herd.

The guys were off the truck and grappling with the little one. They very quickly laid her down on her side, which meant she was safe from harm and out of sight of the matriarch, who had risen and was now ignoring us and heading back to the herd. At that, I let out a very relieved expletive, and Richard laughed.

"Just keep an eye on that cow from up there until we are loaded, Pete," he said.

"Sure."

The box-wagon was soon with us and, as well as keeping an eye on the big cow, I watched a repeat procedure of the elephant-loading from my first day on an elephant catch, when Charlie was driving. Amazingly enough, Charlie had told me of his encounter with an elephant that had also tried to skewer him through the windscreen. I now knew exactly how he must have felt. David had been catching elephant with Richard for two or three years, and I was sure he'd have tales to tell too.

Once the youngster was loaded and safely on the lorry, we again ventured into the herd – this time with much less drama. Still bloody hairy, though, with adrenaline pumping as the cow started heading in our direction again. The banging and shouting did the trick, though, as each time she turned away and followed the herd while we collected another youngster. Once this little girl was loaded, Richard said we had enough for this trip and we headed back to camp. I have to say with some relief; I felt I had had quite a morning.

Back at camp, the little eles were unloaded and settled in. Not too happy at first but they would be much happier the next day. They soon make friends and get used to being waited on.

After lunch, Richard said, "Okay, we are off to Karamoja. Pete, get your gear together – if we are lucky, we can do a catch when we get there."

Well, talk about not resting on your laurels. That was something I had to get used to; the Boss liked to be on the go the whole time. However, it was interesting work, I loved my situation and I wanted to get on top of the job quickly.

'Quickly' was always the operative word and speed was of the essence too, for sure. Once we hit the main road, it was foot down and we were motoring. We headed towards Gulu for a start, then went right, to Lira. We talked all the way, which was good as we talked about the job and what was expected of me. It sounded like fun. Well, we will see, I guess.

Karamoja was quite a dry area, and the camp was quite different from Karuma. However, it was all of a rush, with much shouting from the Boss, making the guys run around, gathering equipment and loading boxes and so on.

"You should be catcher, Pete. Get yourself settled in the catching position," Richard said.

The catching position was standing on the passenger seat and going up through the turret, which would hold me in place.

"I will show you how to use the rope, Pete."

He duly did, and it's simple when you know how, but there was no margin for error. You definitely had to get it right to avoid disasters in the field.

We were soon speeding off to the capture plains, heading well into Karamoja district. This capture was going to be eland, which would be a new learning curve for me. After a short pause to check that the box-wagon was following, we went bush and very soon spotted eland grazing on the plains.

"Get ready, Pete, this is your big moment!" Richard said and, as we zoomed into the herd, the animals all immediately took off.

Richard selected an individual to capture, and in we went. I did what I thought was right, to enable me to drop a noose around the animal's neck, and it went like clockwork; I got one eland in the bag first time. I was pleased, and I knew Richard was too, which was somewhat gratifying. A box was soon dragged off the wagon, the animal treated for internal and external parasites, and then loaded into the box.

We didn't wait for the box to be reloaded but sped off after another animal, with Richard shouting, "Make sure your rope is ready and tied to the vehicle!"

"Sure."

The second capture was the same as the first. Eland run in a straight line, so it's quite a simple operation to keep the rope out of sight of the animal and drop it over its head when the moment seems right. Fantastic! This one too was soon treated and boxed and, once it was loaded onto the box-wagon, we headed back to camp.

When we arrived back at camp, I felt quite tired. Nell van Kamer, a Dutch woman, was the camp manager and I was introduced to her whilst drinking down my tea. She had been out collecting water when we had arrived earlier.

Zapiel was the head domestic here, so I asked him for water to wash and, when it came, it was warm. 'Struth, we get spoiled here! Would you believe a guy was standing by with a towel too?

Richard said, "We need meat. Tomorrow, Pete, maybe you could go out with a couple of the guys and shoot a topi or a hartebeest."

"Yes, sure."

We had a little wander around camp. The main focus appeared to be giraffe. but there were also nice herds of eland, topi and hartebeest. Then came the special ones: roan antelope. What wondrous critters they are! I just got a quick look at them, as the lamps were being lit and darkness was dropping in fast.

We had dinner under our accommodation, as it appeared to be built on stilts. We chatted for a while after we'd eaten, but I'd had quite a day. It was nice to meet Nell and, from what Richard had told me on the way here, she would need me to keep camp accounts fully up to date.

Zapiel showed me where I was to sleep upstairs. Before I went to sleep, I considered everything we'd done that day. I was shattered but still on a high from all the events and activities.

Elephant capture was extremely dangerous, was my first conclusion. Antelope capture is very dangerous, my second conclusion. But wow! What an adrenaline rush. Fear simply gives way to the huge adrenaline flood, which seems to consume the body and mind throughout the dangerous period.

Am I to become an adrenaline junkie? Well, maybe. But for now, sleep is good.

Chapter 9

It was still dark when my cup of tea arrived, and I was more than a little disorientated at first. But I looked up as Zapiel said, "*Habari za asubuhi*."

"Good morning, Zapiel," I said.

"*Chai iko hapa.*"

"Thank you, Zapiel, and a very welcome cup of tea it is too."

I drank my tea and was just climbing into my shorts when I heard groans from the other end of the building, followed by what was to be the Boss's morning rallying call.

"Okay, I'm up, you should all be up!"

A new day and I was a little tired – I had spent most of the night dreaming about capturing elephant and eland. However, I was keen to get downstairs and involved in preparations for our next excursion into the bush.

Today it was going to be my turn to test out my abilities with the rope on the really speedy animals.

Excitement was growing among the catchers too, I could sense it. Richard was barking out commands and I made sure my gear was ready, including a spare bamboo pole on the box vehicle, along with a second length of rope.

I had to make sure my pole was properly assembled, with wire inserted at the end and secured to hold the rope in place, and had enough adhesive tape to stick the rope to the pole long enough to get the noose around the animal's neck. The other end of the rope was tied securely to the truck –

after all, we didn't want an animal charging off through the bush with a rope trailing behind it.

At that point, I realised someone, who I later learnt was a guy called Masabai, was watching my every move.

"*Mzuri?*" I said, pointing at the catch-pole.

"*Ndo kila kitu mzuri, bwana.*" (Yes, everything is good.) He said it with a smile.

We were very soon heading out along the track to the main road and away, with lots of excited chatter from the guys, My leather jacket was zipped up as it was bloody cold at that time of day with the wind chill. Richard slowed and then stopped.

"The box car, is it with us?"

"Yes, coming now," I said.

We turned from the main road and meandered through the bush. There was a great deal of jabber and pointing, as a herd of topi came into view.

"Okay, Pete, ready?"

"Yes."

"Here we go!"

I had the most dangerous position but it was also very much the snug one, as I stood up on the passenger seat with my body going up through the very well-padded turret. It was a home-made version of the Humber truck turrets and it anchored me so well in position that I didn't need to hold on. This left both my hands free, as I needed them to do the rope work, and it also meant that I didn't get thrown around when the vehicle changed course at high speed.

Richard was a great driver, which gave me the confidence to focus on my job. Richard had told me it was extremely important to get the capture of an animal right first time. Fortunately, I was quite strong – a necessity, as I soon found out, for handling the pole through the twists and turns of a chase. A 22-foot catch-pole complete with rope also produces a great deal of drag, and so more than a little effort is necessary to keep the pole ready to strike.

I found I needed more reach and flexibility than standing on the seat allowed me, so I managed to climb onto the back of the seat with only my legs in the turret. It was a little more precarious now, having to rely on my leg and stomach muscles to keep me in the Jeep, but it gave me much more flexibility of movement and close to two-foot more reach.

The topi were tricky little buggers, their speed and agility quite incredible, but I read the situation correctly and had the luck to rope one at my first attempt. We slowed to a stop, the Boss shouted, "*Kamata, kamata, kamata!*" (catch, catch, catch), and the catchers leapt from the truck.

"Keep your rope tight, Pete, so that the guys can get around it safely."

The topi leapt and jumped a little but the guys soon grabbed it and got it under control and safe. While the guys treated the animal for parasites internally and externally, I re-assembled my catch-pole. I took stock of my actions throughout the chase and was content, but I knew that with time, I could improve on my performance.

I climbed down and gave the guys a hand with the loading of the crate onto the box-wagon. Once it was loaded, Richard slapped me on the back and said, with a large grin, "Good one! Let's get another!"

This time, I felt slightly more in control of the catch-pole, so I was happier with my efforts. It was a good feeling for all to go well with the capture, and then to hear *kamata, kamata, kamata,* while I kept the rope tight.

It was so much more difficult to rope topi than it had been roping the eland the day before. Unlike the eland that run in a straight line, these critters bobbed and weaved continually, testing us every step of the way.

Once we had caught and loaded the second crate, and all was secure, Richard said, "Okay, that's it for this morning, Pete!"

Then he shouted, "*Trudi kampi!*" (back to camp) to the guys in the box-wagon, and we set off.

As always, a great day was unfolding as we cruised through the bush.

We had ostrich, eland and giraffe to view en route to the main road, from where we headed home.

Tea awaited us at camp and, after we had unloaded, we got some toast. Zapiel had made bread, remarkably, in an oven he had crafted out of an old paraffin can, which he covered with hot embers from the fire. I was amazed by his abilities and his creativity, especially with so little to work with. The bread was delicious too.

Richard then said, "After you've cleaned up, Pete, you should go and get some meat. Take Masabai with you, he knows the drill."

I drove from camp along with Masabai and two other guys, who I learned were Patrick and Prospare. Masabai, a Kenyan, had worked for the Game Department in Nairobi National Park. He had worked with Richard on several safaris and he was a valuable catcher – one of the hands-on grapplers – and he really was a huge asset. He came to be a good and regular companion to me, and I enjoyed hearing tales from his childhood, his work, and Lang'ata, the Nairobi suburb he called home. I would always try to speak Swahili with him, to help me learn the language; his English was quite good, which was a big advantage when learning.

Patrick came from Bugisu in Uganda, close to Karamoja, and he was a tall man – a little like Mr Universe, with huge muscles. Prospare came from the Congo and he would have been a catcher if he wasn't such a good cook. Again, he wasn't that big but, like all the guys, he was incredibly strong. All the guys in our team were pleasant and very, very capable.

I took direction from Masabai, and we travelled into Karamoja District and a long way away from the capture plains. There we found hartebeest, so I took one – a clean shot – and it dropped like a stone. I had been shooting since I was a young boy. I had been taught by my older brothers who had all done their national service, and had used their skill to provide meat for the table, feeding mother, father and all of us six brothers, of which I was the youngest. It wasn't usual for me to use such a powerful rifle, though; this was a .458, which is basically an elephant gun. The old adage was make sure you use enough gun; well, I surely did that.

The guys went straight to it and cut the animal's throat, which I thought was just to bleed it so that the meat didn't spoil. But I learned from Masabai that the majority of the guys were Muslim and, according to their religion, the animal should die that way. I had never heard of that and had no idea. Education is a wonderful thing.

Back in camp, Zapiel soon organised the guys and the animal was butchered. A leg was heavily salted and hung, for Zapiel to cook for us, and the remainder of the meat was shared between the guys.

It was lunchtime and, despite the hunting expedition, we were served mashed potato, cabbage and spam. I enjoyed it nonetheless.

After lunch, I wandered around the camp and came across piles of acacia that were there for feeding the giraffe. Once the giraffe had stripped the leaves and some bark from the branches, the acacias were taken and put around the perimeter of the camp, providing a thorny barrier as a camp border.

The *bomas* here were very shaded, as it was a very dry, arid area with very little natural shade, save for a couple of large trees at the camp entrance. There was a dry riverbed just behind the accommodation, which separated us from what we called the Karamoja bush. It was a nice camp, although it was very different from Karuma, which was quite lush and green. This camp felt much hotter too.

All the animals in camp looked fit and healthy and even the animals I had roped that morning and the night before seemed to have integrated and settled really well.

Richard was now organising the guys in preparation for the afternoon catch.

"A couple of giraffes this afternoon would be good, Pete," he said.

"Yes," I said. "Do I need anything different from this morning?"

"No, you'll be all right."

The one thing I knew would be useful was a bandana or the likes, as my hair had been whipping my eyes during the catch that morning. Rummaging through my case, I found two handkerchiefs, which I tied together and twisted into a thin length and tied them around my head. Better than nothing.

The guys were then loading giraffe crates onto the box-wagon and, once the crates were secured, we were ready to go.

"Tea first!" Richard said, so we relaxed for a few minutes and savoured our cuppa. Richard said it was important not to go out too soon because of the afternoon heat.

When we were ready, we set off down the track and out to the capture plains.

Giraffe are special animals, with such graceful heads bobbing atop those long necks, and I got the impression that they never really thought we could catch them. Entering a giraffe herd was quite something. Their heads all turned in our direction, with a snooty look down their noses at us. Good, I thought, because they would never hit what we called full gallop, which stresses and exhausts them. We never chased any animal to a flat-out gallop. Rope quickly, or leave them alone.

The giraffe capture was fast-moving and quick-roping. Richard had told me to get the rope well down the neck, as the giraffe have the ability to flick it off. I did that and, as we slowed, so did the giraffe. The guys leapt from the truck to the now familiar shout, *kamata kamata kamata!*

It takes a minimum of five guys to hold a young giraffe; an extra one or two, if available. A huge amount of strength and energy was needed to get the animal boxed and loaded, and the guys certainly had that in abundance. They raised the box in the same way as for the elephants, using wheels and tyres.

The capture of the second giraffe was much like the first but, although I did worry I hadn't got the rope far enough down the animal's neck, I got away with it. I found the capture exhilarating and exciting – as I did for every catch – but the giraffe capture was over so quickly; it only took about 20 to 30 seconds. I loved the speed of the chase as the adrenaline started pumping.

After the unloading back at camp and, of course, tea, Richard announced we should hit the road to Entebbe, and so we did. Never a dull moment!

It was quite a drive in the dark, and I noticed that local drivers seemed to have little knowledge of the headlight dip-switch, or at least if they did, they rarely used it. Richard and I shared the driving, mostly over tarmac roads but with quite a stretch on murrum soil roads, which had become corrugated and gave us a juddering, rough ride and really slowed us down.

We arrived at the Nakiwogo camp late that evening, at around 10pm. I was introduced to Leslie Wilcox, who managed the Nakiwogo Monkey and Bird Camp on the lake shore. He was jolly, and obviously had a good rapport with Richard. Les was from Southampton, as were Richard and his family, and I learnt later that for many years Les had been a friend of the Chipperfield family, so he and Richard had known each other for a long time. He was an older man, and it seemed his position here by the lake suited him well.

Scrambled eggs were soon rustled up, along with tea – all very welcome, as always. We didn't eat big meals out here and I never really felt I needed them. I think the heat dampens the appetite somewhat, and we were also always on the go and too busy, somehow.

It had been another long day and what I really needed was my bed. A metal bowl of warm water helped to take the worst of the grime from my hands, face and upper body, but getting properly clean had to wait until the morning. Sleep was far more important.

Chapter 10

Tea at 6am, wow – that's what you call a lay-in! It was really pleasant alongside Lake Victoria at this time of day, with the sun fast rising and giving me a chance to look around camp.

It was really well laid-out, with a large shaded area with colobus monkeys and lesser spot-nosed monkeys – nice quarters for them too. There was a row of aviaries on the side of camp, much larger than I would have expected, where great crested crowned cranes were housed.

I sat a while and watched, as I was always interested in how birds and animals adapted to living in captivity. It seemed everything was relaxed and, as the keeping staff started their daily routines, there was no sign of panic or agitation from animals or birds.

We had porridge for breakfast, and then Richard said we should go to the bank as soon as it opened.

The lake was just too inviting and we had a very quiet spot along the lake front, so I stripped down to my underpants and waded in. A shock at first, but after a minute or two, the water felt really warm. I didn't venture too far out but swam parallel with the shore, about ten to twelve yards out. Wow, what a great way to start the day.

"No-one else going in?" I said. "Surely you venture in, don't you, Les?"

"No, never," was the reply.

I wandered back to my tent to dry off and get dressed again.

Richard said, "If we get off now, Pete, we can call at the hotel to check for post, and then visit the Game Department before going to the bank. Take your gear with you as we will head off to Karuma from there."

It was another two hours before we were on the road to Karuma. Apart from checking for post, Richard also wanted to phone England. We were three hours ahead so we had a coke at the hotel to kill a little time, as Richard didn't want to call too early.

Ruaza, the Chief at the Game Department, seemed like a very nice man. Richard introduced me, saying that I may visit on his behalf at some stage in the future. Our visit to the bank was quite straightforward too; it was useful for me to know the drill, in case I needed to go to these places on my own in the future.

The road north to Karuma was a really good road, and this time I was awake as we travelled from Entebbe up to Kampala. We drove through a chunk of Kampala, and it was very much a city. We then took the road north, maintaining a good speed. I found it fascinating to see larger plantations of bananas and some other large, well-cultivated areas along the way.

Richard pulled over at one point next to a guy selling fruit, and bought a pineapple. They had been cut with about six inches of stalk still on them, peeled, and cut longways into four, giving a handle to hang onto while we each ate a quarter. It was really good and fresh. Richard also bought several passion fruit, which I had never even seen before let alone knew how to eat. Richard said you had to cut them in half and scoop out the flesh from inside with a spoon. I watched him rub one on his shorts, bite a piece out of it, which he then spat out through the window, squeezed it and suck the contents into his mouth. That caused a giggle between us. I did the same and found the flesh a little sharp, but delicious.

We arrived back in camp and, almost before the vehicle had even stopped, Richard was shouting to the guys to *fanya haraka* (do it quick); we were going bush for a late-afternoon elephant catch.

"*Sisi nakwenda safari sahi!*" (We go on a journey right now.)

This time didn't feel as scary as my first elephant catch: no huge elephants attempting to drag me out of the cab, no attempts to run me through with tusks. However, it was still quite daunting to drive into the back of a herd of elephant. Occasionally, a cow would come and attack the front of the truck but then turn and trundle off to catch up with the herd.

Despite the poor visibility, I had learnt to tell just how close in we were. At one point there were elephants at the side of me, maybe ten or fifteen yards away, and I could see the elephants' backsides quite clearly through the fog-like view in front. We were *really* up close to that herd.

The guys on the back would shout and bang on the truck to keep the herd moving and they would do this even more so if any looked like they may come towards us. Then the hand signal to slow down, and I could just see Richard dropping the noose over the young elephant's head. Richard would shout instructions to me to gradually come to a stop as the herd carried on and left us behind. As usual, the catchers were soon off and controlling the young elephant and laying it down for safety and to keep it out of sight of the herd. Once the elephant was loaded, I always needed to take a deep breath as we ventured in for another capture. No two elephant captures were ever the same.

Elephant capture is up-close and dangerous work. Although the herd is eager to move on away from us, it is important for us to keep them on the move before they realise how inferior we are in relation to them and their capabilities. However, there is no telling how the matriarch will react to our disruption of their daily life, or what she may do. The last thing we wanted was a matriarch to be able to get to the side of our truck; that would not only put the guys in great danger, but she could also hit or lift the vehicle from the side. If we kept on the move, she couldn't do any of that.

On one occasion, we were in danger of being hit broadside so I just had to accelerate while turning away from the herd. That's never a good thing to have to do, as there is always an anthill or a warthog hole you could collide with or drop into. Occasionally, when I did drop into a hole because I just couldn't avoid it, the remark would come: "You've got the whole of bloody Africa out here and you go and drive into a hole!"

Elephant matriarchs were attempting to turn and see us off at every opportunity, which is where the guys' shouting and banging would hopefully intimidate them enough to continue behind the herd. When the matriarchs did turn back, the driver would often be the last to know about it as not only would the air be hanging thick and heavy with dust, but by then the driver would generally be following hand signals. Although instructions were shouted down the roof turret at the driver, it could be difficult to hear over the overall din and the guys on the back shouting and banging the side of the truck.

Often, when I was driving, the first I would know was when I saw that huge shape appearing in front of me and I just knew I would have to keep plenty of power available to push the cow back as she made her attack. On most occasions, she would give way, turning again and following the herd. When the cow did decide to mount the bonnet and clamber towards the driving cab, I would keep my foot on the accelerator to push her back while trying to stay clear of her trunk and tusks. Thankfully, I always managed to turn her like this, and send her on her way. It was a particularly dangerous cow that climbed on the bonnet on my first day out and I felt great relief when she stumbled and fell. (It was also pleasing to know it wasn't just me that dropped into holes!)

Back at camp, once I was nicely soaked and clean, I checked on the young eles that we'd caught. They were looking a little bewildered and weren't eating at that point, but we knew that it would take a couple of days for them to be settled and get into a routine.

After dinner, Richard said we may need a couple of hippos, so we should go out in a couple of hours to see what we could find.

"You can see how we go on, Pete."

We always crammed so much into each day, so I was always looking forward to a bath, food and bed. There was little time for sitting around, so having to wait until 9.30pm and then going bush again, made for a really late night.

This capture trip was a most interesting venture. Hippo spend all day in the water, and then head inland at night to feed on the vegetation, just as the one did that I could often hear munching close to where I slept in Karuma. So the idea is to make the catch before they get back to the water.

We went out in a Toyota Land Cruiser, as it was quieter than the Humber truck and more manoeuvrable, and we found two hippos that we could have caught or at least tried to. We picked them up with a powerful spotlight and we gave a little chase, but this was only so I could see how they ran and see the technique and equipment required.

It was good to see how it was done: speed is of the essence, as they immediately head for water and don't need to go around anything but just plough directly through whatever is in their path. You use a noose in just the same way, but the noose has a bag/sack around it too, so that when you pull the noose tight, there is a bag over the young hippo's head, making the job a little safer for the catchers.

We were out for around an hour and a half, during which time we also spotted two troops of baboons in our spotlight with, in both cases, a leopard close by. Quite a thrill to see leopards, the light just catching their eyes to give them away. This must have been scary for the baboons, that's for sure, and it's something they live with every night. However, when the baboons attack as a troop, they are bloody scary too.

Back in camp it was to be a short night, but first a cup of tea that was, even then, waiting for us.

Chapter 11

In the early days of working at Woburn Safari Park, it was all hands on deck. No-one specialised in working with just one species as they often do today, basically because we were setting up an animal park and nothing was established yet. We all had to work with all the animals and I really enjoyed that. I would work with big cats, but then also with giraffe, wildebeest and elephant one day, and maybe buffalo, baboons and rhino the next.

All of the team at Woburn got on well together and there was a great deal of camaraderie among us as most of us were young and enthusiastic and we learned and gained experience from each other. The park was being built around us and, before it opened to the public, older and more experienced people were drafted in to oversee the staff and the animal accommodation.

I spent a lot of time working with elephants and found them particularly interesting. My first capture trip to Uganda enhanced my love affair with these special animals, and I always considered it a treat to work with them. Over the years, I got to know the Woburn elephants very well. Elephant work is specialised and, although I wasn't an elephant keeper, I would watch the way the staff worked with them.

Strangely enough, I did most of my elephant work when I was a curator. Over the years, I had a number of elephants and elephant-keepers as part of my teams in various establishments, and I had overall responsibility for them and their welfare. When I was curator of two parks at the same time, I had fourteen Asian elephant in one and sixteen African elephant in the other.

Tilly was the first elephant keeper at Woburn. He was from Sri Lanka, and was a very nice guy – he and I got on well together. However, he had to move on, and there were various elephant keepers after him, one of whom was Paul Cooper, who had a lovely relationship with the four elephant cows: Edie, Mary, Rosey and Gulu (although people tended to call her Gula). I would be in the elephant house almost every morning with him, but Paul preferred to work alone. He'd take the animals out to the park for the day, and then return to complete their housework, making up feeds, taking hay to his elephants, and then spending time with them. I learned a great deal from just watching him. However, when he also had to leave us at short notice for personal reasons, I felt I needed to fill the void myself, until others were able to take over.

I would meet and greet the elephants every morning and take them out to their enclosure. I would give them hay and branches when I could get them, and then would leave others to clean up the house and prepare the feeds while I resumed my duties as curator. When time allowed, I would walk the eles up through the picnic area and past visitors. Anne Stewart, Head of Rhino, Giraffe, etc., would accompany me as my back-up.

At first, the eles were reluctant, not really sure and a bit shy about walking so close to the visitors. The area was new to them too, so if there was a hand on Edie's trunk, they felt they could put their trust in us and walked on nicely, out of the park and through the estate woodland. We had fun and the eles loved it! They were soon very much in their element, stealing tree branches to munch on as we walked; they knew they shouldn't, but being allowed to get away with it was a real treat for them!

I learnt that it takes time for keepers and elephants to get to know each other, but once the bond is set, it is a very rewarding situation all round. Initially, as you would do with your dog, you need to show your authority over the elephants by telling them off or maybe giving them the odd clip. It's nothing painful but a merely show of displeasure, and they do understand what it means. They are very intelligent animals and understand far more than we realise.

In my opinion, there are two main positions within an elephant herd: lead cow (the boss), who will determine where the herd will go, stop, feed, and so on, even though elephants feed continually, snatching at tasty-looking foliage as they travel. Elephants are like baling machines; loose food fed into the front and solid bales drop out of the back-end.

The second position is the matriarch, or the policeman, of the herd. She will do the lead cow's bidding, and all will obey her. A natural babysitter, she will also tend to the youngsters within the herd. It would appear that maybe a barren female assumes this role within the herd.

That is why it is so important to be strict when you work with elephants. Pathetic humans are no match for elephants, if they feel they can challenge for leadership.

Once you've established leadership as a keeper, the herd will regard you as the lead or matriarch elephant, and they will put great trust in you. When they encounter something strange, or something that they don't understand, they will follow you, putting their full trust in you. This bond and trust should never be abused.

When you have developed this close bond with the elephants, there are many fun times to be had. I would always greet every elephant individually when I entered their house each morning. Occasionally, I would ignore one and walk by, only to find a trunk wrapped around my arm, and I'd be pulled back in front of the animal. At that, I would make an extra fuss of her and stay a little longer with her.

When one cow had damaged an ankle/fetlock joint, which then became infected, she needed treatment twice a day. It was painful for her while I treated her, as I needed to flush the hole, which tracked all the way down to the bone. As I knelt down to attend to her wound, she would tuck her trunk under and put it against my head; as the pain grew, so did the pressure on my head, and when it got to the point where it was too much for me to bear, I knew she had had enough.

Very occasionally, when I was filling a water trough with a hose, and an elephant came over to drink, I would squirt water into her face and she would pull back. She would attempt this several times and, eventually, I would let her slide her trunk into the trough to have a drink. Once the trunk was nice and full, I would get the water full-bore in the face!

I was once under attack from a rhino while walking the elephants out to their enclosure. The rhino's name was Sherman, after the tank, and he appeared very much to be on a mission. As he got to within ten to twelve yards of us, Edie, the elephant herd's leading cow, dropped her head and came up under Sherman's chin, flicking him a full 180 degrees and setting him off running in the opposite direction. He never even looked back.

Elephant work is probably the most rewarding of occupations, and you grow to love your charges and can often feel their love. I was never a trainer of elephants, just a keeper who enjoyed working with them. It is always very important to remember, though, that just like humans, not all elephants will like you or want to be friendly with you.

Chapter 12

Back in Africa, it was to be buffalo for today's morning foray into the bush.

The Humbers were a treat to drive as they seemed to be able to cope with any terrain. The Rolls Royce engine just purred, providing bags of power when needed, and it was equipped with four-wheel drive capacity should we need it. The downside was that reverse gear automatically put the vehicle into four-wheel drive but there was a lump on the side of the gear stick which knocked the four-wheel drive lever into play each time reverse was engaged. Thankfully someone, probably David, had taken a hacksaw to it so that it missed the four-by-four lever.

Buffalo tend to run in a straight line, but they close ranks and run in a huddle, so it can be difficult to capture the single animal you've selected. In the end, many will fit the bill, so you drop the noose over the one that's nearest. Once we'd got the noose around the neck, and we were slowing to a halt, we needed to know the rest of the herd had continued on its way, so I'd then block their view with the truck so we could operate in relative safety.

They are certainly fiery animals, often bouncing and attempting to gore the catchers. That day, we collected two animals, with Richard directing me and doing the catching himself. Once we'd loaded them, we dispatched the box-wagon back to camp, then we slowly cruised around until we found a reedbuck, which Richard shot for the pot.

Back at camp, tea was very welcome and then a strip, wash, teeth and so on.

Karuma camp was quite close to the Nile, and all around the river it was very lush and green. Although life was hectic, with Richard pushing us to be on the go all the time, if we had an hour or two of downtime, the camp was a tranquil place to relax. After that morning capture of two young buffalo, Kambanyoka, our cook and head domestic, asked if I wanted to go fishing with him. (Kambanyoka's name meant 'rope-snake', and I called him Kambanyok for short. But not very.)

In the warm sun, we drove down one of our tracks to the Nile, with Ugandan kob sprinting from our path and reedbuck skulking in the long grass, hoping we wouldn't notice them. Near the Nile, we veered slowly off the track. Kambanyok stood on the passenger seat, directing me so we didn't drop into a warthog hole or collide with an anthill. I parked, and we walked the last 30 yards.

Our equipment included a stick for a rod, a small metal can, and a large paraffin container. We stopped at a small inlet to the river and Kambanyok started digging in the soft ground for worms, which he dropped into the small metal can. I just sat and watched the professional at work. He quickly collected about a dozen worms before we moved on.

Once we got to the river, he wasted no time in filling the paraffin can with water, applying worm to hook, and dropping the hook just six feet from the edge. No sooner had the hook hit the water than he pulled it up, flicking the small fish onto land, and dipping the hook back into the water with the worm still intact. I grabbed the small fish in cupped hands and only just managed to put it into the paraffin can before the next one was flicked from the water. The third time, the fish took the bait so there was a short delay while Kambanyok removed it from the hook. Once he'd applied a new worm and put the line back in, I was scurrying after another little chap as it arrived on the bank. Just one more catch and we were on the move again, with me carrying the can of little swimmers.

I'd never been much of a fisherman, apart from catching the odd stickleback or minnow in the local pond or stream as a kid, so I found it fascinating to watch an expert at work. At our next stop, Kambanyok made himself comfortable alongside the Nile; comfortable, I certainly was not. I'd seen plenty of hippos in the river and crocodiles on the banks, just waiting for a thirsty mammal to come down to the water's edge, so I was on high alert. I had to have a little walk along the bank in each direction to assure myself I wasn't about to be eaten!

This time, Kambanyok used the small fish as bait, and it wasn't long before he pulled up his line. I could hardly believe the size of the perch attached. I watched Kambanyok quickly despatch the fish, and cast again. There wasn't the boredom, as in England, of sitting on cold river banks for hours in the hope of catching a little fish. We quickly got what we came for, and this was another great example of how adept my African colleagues always were. Kambanyok was so at one with his surroundings, with great knowledge of how to live from the land, yet only taking from it what was necessary.

When he'd caught four large fish, Kambanyok told me to have a try, and so it was that I caught a huge perch. It was about two feet long, ten inches deep, and the only fish I've ever caught in my life, but hey, what a fisherman's tale!

As we were packing up to leave, there was a rustling in the bush close by and a young bull elephant came trundling out, causing more than a little panic. I ran to the nearest tree – a small and spindly specimen that would have fallen over if the animal even just leant against it – and Kambanyok stood as still as a statue until danger had passed. We were lucky the animal was alone and content to continue on its journey; normally, only a large bull elephant travels alone. Elephants always stay with the herd but I think the adult females in the herd must have put this guy in his place, probably because of attempted sexual activity. Definitely time for us to move on, though, as others might be following.

Back at camp, Kambanyok and Ndenaza prepared the fish and battered it for a great lunch. After lunch, Richard said we should go down to Entebbe, as Ann was going bring a young elephant down to Nakiwogo the following day, to be delivered to Nairobi.

"Can I leave you to take the elephant to Nairobi, Pete? I need to be back at home for a couple of days," Richard said, as we drove.

"Yes, sure."

Well, that should be an experience, I thought.

It is quite a run between camps, and when we arrived in Nakiwogo, Richard told Les we would be staying at the Lake Vic Hotel in Entebbe that night and invited him to come and join us for dinner.

We got our rooms at the hotel and I immediately ran a bath, where I wallowed for a good hour before putting on my jeans and long-sleeved shirt. That was me clean and dressed.

I wandered downstairs and was having a drink, when Les arrived and we sat and talked until Richard arrived. Les was a nice man, and we got along very well. He'd done a lot of work with birds, and he was one of the first to breed macaws in the UK. He specialised in the parrot-type birds and indeed had an African Grey parrot in his camp, which would wander around with him.

We had a nice dinner and a pleasant evening, with many laughs and all very jovial. But my bed was beckoning, so once I'd asked what time we needed to meet in the morning, I departed to bed.

It was to be a lay-in the next morning, if I wanted it; nice thought, but the body gets used to a routine, and 5am was when my body would come alive. I could never see the point in lying in bed if not asleep, so I got up. It was just starting to get light, so I wandered out of the hotel and along the road. Life is so different in the early morning, which is my favourite time of day.

It was around 6.45am when I returned to the hotel and the dining room was open, so I wandered in and sat down. Almost immediately, Lassie, the head waiter, arrived, and I wondered if he ever had a day off. I ordered tea and said I would wait for Richard to arrive before eating. The tea arrived and so too did Richard. I had an omelette, nicely cooked, with some toast, while Richard had boiled eggs and toast; all very nice.

On the way down to camp, Richard told me the people in Nairobi would be expecting the elephant that I was to take there the following day. He also told me that a plane was being organised to collect the twenty-five elephant to go to America and we would have full details within the next few days.

We spent that day in Nakiwogo camp, and I was preparing myself for the Nairobi trip. I certainly needed to dress properly for the city, in jeans and shirt, and not the shorts and old T-shirts that were my usual attire.

Ann arrived mid-afternoon with the elephant, and final preparations were made to keep the elephant happy and healthy throughout its trip. Richard told Ann that as soon as he had more details, he would let her know so she could organise to get the twenty-five elephant from Karuma down to Nakiwogo, ready for their departure to America.

During the evening, we took Richard to the airport to fly back to England, then took dinner at the hotel again. This was almost civilised!

I left for Nairobi the following morning at around 6am and, I have to say, the VW pick-up I had to drive looked very top-heavy with the young elephant on the back. Masabai came with me as usual; he lived in the area we were going to and wanted to make a family visit. It was a slow trip, and the pick-up laboured a little on occasion.

Going through customs at the Uganda/Kenya border with a young elephant was entertaining for the officers, and created much interest for anyone around at that time. However, all of our paperwork was in order, so all went smoothly and we proceeded on our way without any trouble.

It was a lovely trip, offering such stunning views as we climbed the escarpment, with glimpses of the beautiful Rift Valley, as well as the lakes Navasha, Elmenteita, and Nakuru.

Masabai, knowing the area well, guided me to the drop-off farm where a small welcoming committee greeted us on our arrival. There was a very smart, good-looking blonde lady, who quickly greeted me.

"Just get out and leave the vehicle," she said. "They will see to it. Come in and have a drink. What would you like, beer or soft drink?"

"Soft drink, please," I said.

"Orange all right?"

"Yes, thank you."

"Do sit down."

I did. It was a lovely, spacious, colonial-type house with comfortable, large furnishings and it was totally spotless. The lady came into the room with a glass of orange juice, and I was very ready for that but not for what came next. She wore a white, body-hugging dress over her near-perfect figure, and it sat some four inches above the knee. She handed me the glass, and positioned herself opposite me on a settee, making polite conversation, asking me how long it had taken me to do the trip, where the animal had been caught and so on. All the time, putting her knees together, knees apart. As I sipped my drink politely, I thought grief, she'd be showing me her knickers next.

Like a lightning bolt, bang! What knickers? I tried hard to look away, and found myself gulping down my drink.

"More?" she said.

"Yes, please," I said, confused in my head as to what I was wanting more of.

I had been in the bush for months, so this moment required from me very much-needed composure and a great deal of self-control.

When what now appeared to me to be a very beautiful woman entered the room once more, with my second glass of orange juice, I felt that deep-down stirring within my loins. I was a young country boy in a strange situation, and I recognised my fear of this apparently fast woman, so I leapt to my feet, thanked her for the drinks and suggested we check the progress of the elephant unloading.

Many thoughts rushed through my head as we moved towards the door, many not making for gentlemanly conduct. I was aware of the so-called 'man-eaters' in the bush, but I didn't know they'd be here in Nairobi; either this lady was looking for fun, or I could have completely misunderstood the situation and it could all have been a great mistake. Perhaps she never wore knickers at all. What madness! What was I thinking? Surely it was all pretty obvious what was afoot. I suppose it was my upbringing that kicked in at that point, where discretion is the better part of valour and all that. Gentlemanly conduct was guaranteed never to get me laid.

With my head buzzing and many erotic thoughts running through my mind, I drove into Nairobi and checked into the Hilton Hotel. We always did that when we were in town, so people would know where to find us should they need us. The next day, I went shopping for supplies, met up with Masabai, and we returned to Uganda.

The following day, when I met Richard off his evening flight to Entebbe, I related the tale of my visit to Nairobi. He laughed, and said he'd heard similar stories before.

"So you had a lucky escape?" he said.

"Yes," I said.

"You *did* escape, didn't you?"

"Yes."

"Sure?"

"Yes, sure."

It had been a hell of a temptation, and she must have thought there was something really wrong with me to walk away like that. I'm not sure I'd made the right decision; they do say, a little of what you fancy does you good.

As anticipated, we soon headed off to Karamoja and, although we would arrive late, we'd be all set for an early catch the next morning.

Chapter 13

Up and at it early, we captured two hartebeest and one beautiful roan antelope the next day. They led us a bit of a dance but we had become really quite proficient by then.

When we got back to camp, we offloaded the morning's catch, drank tea, and then I cleaned myself up. It was then decided that we needed meat, so I called the guys together and we went bush. I just loved cruising around in an open-topped Jeep with the sun beating down on me, air rushing past and through the cab. The guys would stand on the back to make the most of it too.

We found another hartebeest and, once I'd shot it, the guys rushed in to cut the animal's jugular vein. The animal had died instantly, but even when animals are slaughtered at an abattoir, it's standard practice to bleed the animal out or the meat will spoil. (It is not really something you'd think about when you're tucking into your Sunday roast, is it?)

I much preferred capture to shooting, as I wasn't keen on the carnage, but with no butcher's shops around, we had to fill the void ourselves. I always took pride in my ability with a rifle; apart from using it to obtain meat, the rifle was for our protection too, and I never took a shot at an animal unless I felt sure I'd hit my mark. A good teacher ensures their pupils learn to look beyond their target, as bullets can go through the target too, so you never shoot an animal that is part of a group, only one that's on the edge of a group – one on its own is always better.

We got back to camp in time for lunch, which was meat stew and chips – I loved it. The meat was lean and extremely tender, as was all of our meat;

game meat has very little fat on it. Our newly-acquired hartebeest meat would first need to be butchered and heavily salted, and then allowed to hang for a few days. You need to hang meat for a while before you eat it, as that gives the muscle time to relax, making the meat more tender.

After lunch, it was back to the bush for the afternoon catch, which was all but a replay of the morning's catch: two hartebeest and another lovely roan antelope. After the unloading back at camp, Richard said perhaps we should get back to Entebbe, ready for the elephant shipment, so we loaded our gear and left for Entebbe.

We arrived late at Nakiwogo, and saw that the elephant crates had been lined up, so it was all clearly happening the next day. After the kitchen staff had produced another omelette for us, I needed my bed. It had been another long day, so quick hands, face and teeth job after eating, and I was gone.

Knowing the animals had all arrived safely from Karuma, we had to assemble them at the airport, ready for loading onto a McDonnell Douglas DC8 plane that was flying in that day. It took quite a lot of time to transport the elephants to the airport.

One thing that has always amazed me is just how quickly elephants appear to convert food into manure: no sooner has the food entered one end than it is discharged from the other. You can imagine, then, that with a growing number of elephants waiting at the airport, we were feeding, watering and cleaning up, non-stop, just to keep the area clean! The food is not digested that fast really, it's just seems that way as elephants never seem to stop eating!

In the bush, an elephant's diet is high in fibre and low in protein, and it can take between eighteen and twenty-four hours to digest its good fully. Juvenile elephants, as we had, generally need a daily feed of about sixty pounds of feed (for their body weight, which at our best guess was around a ton), but we had introduced them to a locally-made cattle cake, which reduced the volume of food required for their journey.

When we'd managed to get about eighteen of the animals to the airport,

Richard said he thought something was going on, as a number of military vehicles seemed to be converging on the airport. We decided we should make a hasty retreat to camp and, as we did so, we met a convoy heading into the airport. General Idi Amin, the then President of Uganda, was actually driving the first Jeep, followed by vehicles full of army personnel. It looked to us like there was a coup brewing.

When we got back to camp, we speculated about what would happen next. If it was indeed a coup, then the airport would be out of bounds, the DC8 would either have to divert or land in the middle of it, and we'd have to get the elephants out and back to camp somehow.

From our camp on the shores of Lake Victoria, we could see the end of the airport runway quite clearly. There was a stationary plane on the runway, and we saw a tank trundle down and stop in front of it. One of our guys, who'd been left to look after the animals, came jogging into camp and told us the plane was in fact a hijacked plane, and it had landed to refuel.

We were all relieved, but felt for those on board experiencing such a scary situation. After about twenty minutes, people started pouring out of the plane; they looked like ants exiting one of the many anthills you'd see dotted about the African landscape. We learnt later that Idi Amin had told the hijackers that if they didn't give themselves up, he'd blow the cockpit apart. It was a huge relief it hadn't actually come to that.

I've since learnt that it was an Ethiopian couple aboard the 31-seater aircraft – an East African Airways Fokker Friendship, en route from Nairobi to Malindi – who had ordered the pilot to take them to Moscow via Libya. Because the aircraft had a limited range, the pilot had had to refuel in Entebbe, where Amin took control of the situation. This all took place on the 20th of March, 1974.

Without a word, but all deep in thought, we got back to work, taking the remaining elephants to the airport. We had a job to do, after all. By the time we got to the airport, the DC8 charter plane had landed and was standing close by. We spent the next few hours putting down plastic sheeting and manually hauling the crates into the aircraft, as there were no pallets available. It was tedious, back-breaking work, and required all hands on deck.

The crates were heavy enough, with each containing a four-year-old elephant. We were a team of eight or ten guys, if we could all get around the crate, and we were all lifting and shunting, trying not to tear the plastic sheeting, otherwise the urine would have seeped through. As careful as we tried to be, there were many tears and scuffs in the plastic sheeting.

Soon after I arrived in Africa, the guys had shown me how to lift and shift weight: by lifting and pushing against each other, then trying to move in the right direction. I was quite strong, but I felt like I was the weakling of the bunch. We each had to lift and shift 300 pounds or more, even though it began to feel like each elephant weighed about ten tons, but we managed to get all twenty-five animals onto the aircraft, along with the smell of elephant pee and dung! The plane would be filled with that stench for the nine-hour flight to the UK and the next nine- or ten-hour flight to the US, and perhaps even forever more.

I could just imagine the cargo handlers at Heathrow Airport, with all the health and safety regulations they had to deal with, when they learnt we had loaded all of the elephants by hand at this end!

It was around midnight by the time we got back to camp and, to say we were grubby, was a vast understatement. We all smelt like elephant and we knew we would until we were able to soak in a nice warm bath.

We managed a few hours of sleep, before returning to the airport to watch the aircraft take off at 5am. Because of the weight of its cargo, the plane had to take off early to get enough lift to leave the ground. High temperatures thin the atmosphere and spread the oxygen molecules further apart from one another, so with fewer air molecules pushing back beneath the wings of the plane, the air fails to generate enough force for take-off.

I watched with interest and some anxiety as the plane trundled down the runway, discharging clouds of black smoke as it slowly climbed skywards. And then they were off! Our job was done, and I looked forward to another wonderful day in Africa.

We spent the rest of that day in Nakiwogo. A long swim in the lake got rid of a great deal of the elephant smell and, later that afternoon after a visit to the bank and the Game Department, we went to the hotel. We got a room, just to get clean, and I got to go first for a good soak. Once I felt clean and looked a little more respectable, I went downstairs and Richard went up for his chance to clean up.

Richard, Les and I then took dinner at the hotel, and Richard announced that he and Les would be going back to the UK the following day, as Les had to take care of some personal matters.

"Perhaps you could check out the sawmill at Budongo tomorrow, after you drop us at the airport, Pete?" Richard said.

"Yes, sure." That had become my standard answer.

We spent the night at Nakiwogo and I dropped Richard and Les at the airport the following morning. When I pulled up outside the airport, Richard and Les got out of the vehicle and Richard did his usual – he got out, said, "See you anon", slammed the door and never once looked back. Les turned and waved as he walked into the airport building.

I don't know what it was about looking back; Richard would never do it. Equally, if he were to forget something, he would never go back for it as he'd consider he'd be tempting fate. On one occasion, when he and I flew up to Nairobi together, he stopped as we walked through arrivals and said he'd left his leather jacket on the plane. He then just carried on walking. I said I'd go back for it and he said, "No, it's gone now, don't worry about it." It was a really good leather jacket too and I would have loved to have owned it, but he would never go back for anything. On his next trip back to England, he bought another leather jacket, which was nothing like as good as the one he'd left on the plane.

Arrival in Kilindeni Mombasa

Giraffe train ride

Home in Karamoja

Diani Beach Mombasa

Ostrich chicks Karamoja

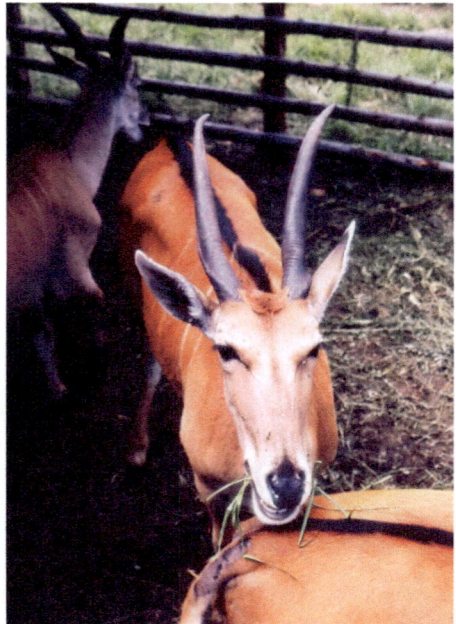

Eland in boma, photo by Kit Thackeray

Crate training giraffe

First giraffe that I caught without Richard

Giraffe on board ship

Chapter 14

It started with a smile. She was at the bar with people who I assumed to be her Aeroflot colleagues – a pilot, a first officer and another cabin crew member, was my guess. I was sitting in the corner of the bar room, facing the door. I was back in the Lake Victoria Hotel because I'd been checking out the sawmill and the timber supplies for building animal crates, as Richard had asked me to do.

I was hoping to meet up with a pilot called Paddy Riley (I feel he should have been Patrick O'Riley but no-one ever called him that), who flew his own charter plane. Richard had introduced me to him, as he'd been pivotal in rescuing a colleague, Mike, following an accident in the bush at Karamoja. Mike had been taken to Mount Elgon Hospital and was in grave danger of losing a leg, but doctors were refusing to discharge him to go elsewhere. Paddy flew into a small airstrip close by and, after what was all but a kidnap operation by Richard and co, Paddy flew Mike to Nairobi for treatment there, before returning him to the UK, where they managed to save his leg.

I always enjoyed chatting to Paddy whenever I got the opportunity. He was an old-school colonial type, very much living in the past, and he had such great tales of times gone by. I found them interesting and very entertaining, but mostly they made me feel I'd been born too late. He'd talk about times when the hotel bar would have been buzzing with air crews from around the world, as well as hunters, tea planters, coffee growers, and many other local colonial characters. Now, it appeared only the Russian carrier, Aeroflot, had regular flights to Entebbe; at least they were the only crews I would see when visiting for a meal or on the occasions when only a hot bath would put the world to rights.

At 7.30 each evening, I'd also see a couple of elderly colonials come in – right on cue – for just the two drinks, and then they'd depart. I thought they must be brothers, as they were always spotless in appearance, shorts two inches above the knee, with short-sleeved shirts, all matching. We always referred to them as 'the two *mzungus*' (white guys) – not the correct way to speak, as it should have been *wazungu mbile*. These days, of course, I might have other ideas about the nature of their relationship.

As time was passing, I decided to wander through to the dining room as it felt like it was time to eat. That same girl smiled again and nodded as I passed the group of them at the bar.

In the dining room, Lassie, the head waiter, came over and greeted me and asked after Richard. I explained that he'd gone back to England and that I had Uganda to myself, which raised a smile from him.

After a few minutes, the Russian crew arrived and sat down to eat, and I had a clear view of that girl, as she sat at the table in a position opposite me. Every time I glanced up, her eyes seemed to be piercing into me, so I just smiled and looked away.

The hotel didn't always have a full menu, as times were difficult, but Lassie's recommendations were always good. Dinner for me was just a main meal, no trimmings or starters or desserts. A good steak was my preference, when it was available, and indeed on this evening it was. I would always have it well done (just in case of kitchen contamination) and with a pepper sauce. It wasn't better than camp food but different somehow.

Having cleaned my plate, I called Lassie over, paid my bill and, as instructed by Richard, I always left Lassie a generous tip too. I then wandered back to the bar to see if Paddy had turned up, but no, he still hadn't. I ordered a coffee and sat a little longer.

Suddenly that girl was standing next to my table. She smiled and asked if she could sit with me.

"Sure," I said. "Would you like a drink?"

"Yes, please. I would like vodka."

Wow! Okay, well just the one, I thought. None of the capture team were drinkers, but I would have the odd drink on occasion. Once, when visitors to our Karamoja camp left some Uganda *waragi*, I tried a drop of that but I wasn't impressed. I'm sure you could get a fire going with it. I would sometimes have a Bells beer in the Lake Vic, or a Tusker beer in Nairobi at the Long Bar, part of the New Stanley Hotel. (A colleague once commented that there were more elephants shot in that bar than in the whole of Africa!)

I asked the girl if they were flying out the following day or if they were in Entebbe for a couple of days.

"We fly tomorrow, but only to Nairobi where we stop over, returning to Moscow the following day."

How strange, I thought.

"So," I said, "if I were going to fly with you to Moscow or any other destination other than Kenya, I would need to sleep over there before setting off on my journey again?"

"Yes."

She then went on to tell me the airline's main business was safari holiday passengers from Moscow to Nairobi, and the extension was more of a courtesy for local people travelling between Kenya and Uganda, although a few people did take safaris in Uganda. I do tend to over-think things, but I imagined that that flight would be useful for the locals as normally only East African Airways did that trip.

Her English was very good. I'm always in awe of how other nationals speak English and any other language with such ease. My Swahili was coming on nicely, but it was what was termed 'up-country Swahili', which was what all but officialdom seemed to speak.

Her drink arrived while I was quizzing her and, while we talked, I had a chance to look her over and I liked what I saw. Her hair was dark brown; I thought she was a very good-looking woman, although I remember thinking she could do with a bit of sun.

"What's your name?" I said.

"Olga," she said, putting emphasis on the second syllable.

"Well, nice to meet you, Olga. I'm Pete."

After chatting for a while, Olga asked if I'd like to have a drink with her in her room. I'm sure we both knew what that could lead to.

"Yes please!" I actually shouted that a bit too quickly, hoping I hadn't sounded too over-enthusiastic. We hurried up the stairs.

Olga certainly wasn't backward in coming forward. Once I had bounced through the shower and landed on the bed, détente was soon achieved (the easing of hostility or strained relations), and I felt very much enslaved for the next hour or so. She was pretty dominant, and she had a great deal to be proud of. I wish all of my education had been this much fun!

I crawled into the shower again just after midnight and then we said our farewells.

"Catch you next time," Olga said.

Sure. 'Catch' was the right word; like a fly into a web.

I left, and wound my way around town and back down to Nakiwogo and thought about the great life we had out here, doing what we did and, for the most part, we were happy. My time in Africa always felt like how I'd imagined Eden to be, and there was no point being in the Garden of Eden if you didn't taste the fruits. That was my theory, anyway.

Back at camp, and with great relief, I climbed into bed, where I stayed until around 8am the next morning. I had eggs on toast for breakfast, had a very relaxing day, and I even swam in the lake for a while. The Boss was due back the following evening and I knew life would pick up pace considerably as soon as he got back.

I was right. I met Richard at the airport around 8.30pm off the 7pm flight from Nairobi; he had eaten on the plane, so we just hit the road for Karamoja. It was a long journey, followed by a short sleep, and up again for the 5am catch. Back to our normal pace.

When we were back in the Lake Victoria Hotel about three weeks later, Lassie told us Paddy had taken his plane up and crashed it on the end of the runway the day after I had been at the hotel. He did always go on about the way the country had deteriorated, but I clearly had no comprehension of the turmoil there must have been in his mind.

It was very sad news indeed; no more seeing Paddy sitting on a stool at the end of the bar. He was a true character, and I still think about him from time to time.

Chapter 15

I knew my time in Uganda was drawing to a close, and I couldn't believe how much I had learned and discovered in the few short months since my arrival. My life out here was so very different from my life back home.

Without a doubt, we led one hell of a hectic life. I can't imagine how many miles we would have travelled in any given week. As you can imagine, we got to know the roads really well – long stretches of tarmac, which were wonderful, interspersed with murrum soil roads. There was a certain joy in arriving at the murrum soil stretch of road, and finding it had been graded by a huge levelling machine; this gave us a comfortable road to drive on, as opposed to the horrific corrugations we most often had to endure.

However, it all suited me well. When we were not travelling at night, which we often were, travel was interesting; great countryside and landscapes to view, forests and plains, seeing the soil colour change from dark, rich, almost black cotton-soil to a much lighter brown as we travelled east. I'd also often wonder where all the people were going to or coming from, when we passed them along the roadside.

The capture work gave me, a young man, the thrill of the chase (I believe it was a basic human instinct coming to the fore) but without the carnage. Soon after we'd arrive at camp, and while it was still being set up for the safari, the capture plains were selected. Richard would take the guys out and they would burn large, flat areas that would not only give us better vision of the animals in the area, but would also promote new grass growth that would encourage animals onto our catching plains.

Capturing ostriches was a challenge, as much as it was capturing giraffe. The capture rope needed to be dropped over the animal's head and all the way down the neck to the shoulders, or they would simply flick the rope off. Ostriches, in fact, were better at it than the giraffe were. When they did that, they would then run in a straight line for a while and then drop a wing and, by doing so, change direction by 45 degrees.

Richard's ability behind the wheel was second to none but even he would sometimes come a poor second, as the vehicle simply didn't have the tight turning ability to stay with the ostrich. The object of the exercise for us was to zoom in, drop the rope over the bird quickly before it had a chance to drop a wing and make that 45 degree turn.

The speedy critters were always a challenge on the catching plains. They'd dodge and weave, slow down and speed up, always testing our abilities at every opportunity. Their prime objective was to create enough space to turn more sharply than we could, and create enough distance between us and them to return to the herd.

It was a much easier operation for us to catch ostrich chicks. Often, several broods would be wandering together and, at our approach, the adults would run and the chicks would drop to the ground. They weren't that easy to spot but our eyes soon became accustomed to what we were looking for, and the catchers' eagle eyes missed very little. When that happened, we could collect ten to fifteen chicks at a time, and this was normally all we required.

We would also have to keep a wary eye open for the adults, should they return. Humans are not a good match for ostriches out in the open. If all else fails, it's better to lie down flat and be trampled on than to stand and be ripped open by their huge claw-like toes. Fortunately, we always managed to avoid any confrontation.

It was very important to get control of the animals as soon as we could after we'd roped them, with the Boss's familiar cry of *kamata, kamata, kamata* or, for the horned critters, *kamata pembe* (catch the horn). The horned animals could inflict serious injury, as they have such incredible power and energy. We had to grab and control their horns quickly, and learned to never underestimate the damage they could do.

Jackson's hartebeest (the sub-species in Karamoja) and topi challenged us with their speed and agility. Then there were the roan antelope, my favourite and the most beautiful antelope of all, with their lovely coats and long ears, and they could turn on a sixpence. Eland capture was comparatively slow and, because they run in a straight line like giraffe do, they were among the easiest to capture.

All of these animals would use speed and a great deal of cunning to try and evade capture. After all, we were the enemy, and they assumed they would be killed if caught. Their flight and agility would be their only hope against a predator, or indeed numerous predators, as with a lion-hunting party. I found it impossible to do the work we did without gaining huge admiration for the animals we caught – they were top-class athletes, one and all.

For all of our capture safaris, we'd split our time between the three camps: Karamoja and Karuma, which were our capture camps, and Nakiwogo, which was very much a holding station. I loved all the camps, and enjoyed spending time in them. Ann was a first-class camp manager at Karuma, so very capable and conscientious. She would come on our capture forays for elephant and buffalo, and managed to fit these in between her normal duties.

Time spent with Ann was always an education, a good grounding. She had a great understanding of her role in the bush and of the guys, who would seemingly do anything for her; her Swahili was good and she made sure the whole camp ran like clockwork. Nell was also very competent and kept a great camp at Karamoja, but I spent far less time with her, just down to circumstances really.

One night in Karuma, I woke up, scratching and slapping at various irritations, and then realised my bed had been invaded by an army of soldier ants. I struggled from beneath my mosquito net and blanket, and the ants were everywhere! They were crawling in my hair, and talk about ants in your pants! I ripped my pants off and beat myself with them in order to displace the ants. I must have made quite a fuss, as half the camp arrived to watch as the naked *mzungu* performed the ant dance!

Kambanyok came to my rescue and sorted out my bed, while I ran a comb through my hair time and again to ensure I had dislodged all the ants. Not a good experience for me, but I know I provided many a chuckle in the camp. At least hurricane lamp light isn't as bright as an electric light, but enough that I had little left to hide.

One afternoon, when Ann went out to collect grass and the cutters, she learnt that a python had coiled itself around one of the cutters while he was cutting grass. It was intent on constricting to squeeze the life out of him before consuming him. However, the other cutters had been quick to act, attacking the snake with their *pangas*, literally cutting it off him and killing it.

They brought the snake back to camp and laid it out, and it measured sixteen foot six inches (just over five metres) in length. I didn't see it loaded on their vehicle, but several of the guys would have to have been involved to get it on top of the loaded grass. It wouldn't have been like lifting a bulk lump because it's long and stretchy, but I'd imagine it weighed a couple of hundred pounds. They don't come much bigger than that one. It was a super specimen – female, I think – with beautiful markings, but sadly she chose poorly from a vast African menu.

The man who'd had the close encounter with death then spent the next two days with a *mganga* (a witch doctor – traditional healer or medicine man) because he believed he was due to die. His hope was that the medicine man could help him avoid an early death.

Another time, an army colonel came into the camp at Karamoja, just being nosy, I think. He stayed for a cup of tea with Richard, Nell and myself, and then told us what bad people the Karamojong were. He related how they had been stealing cattle from across the border and now they had large numbers of them up in the hills. He said he was going to take a squadron of men up there and get their cattle back. He told us we should go along for a bit of sport.

"Ah," Richard said, "we are just so busy. We have transport organised, aircraft flying in, so we have a great deal to do."

"Well, at least let me show you some of our fire power," the colonel said. "Come with me, not far, and we will demonstrate."

Neither of us was keen, but Richard felt we should humour him as he was friendly, and friendly Ugandan army officers were few and far between.

The colonel drove off in his convoy of three army Jeeps, and we followed. It wasn't far down the road when we veered off to the right and stopped. They lifted a large metal container from one of the Jeeps and took out a bazooka. I had only seen them in war films but knew it was quite a lump of hardware.

It was then mounted on a sergeant's shoulder, and he kept moving right to left. I knew we shouldn't be in front or behind such a thing, but until we knew which way he would point it to fire it, I was somewhat nervous. I didn't realise it had to be loaded from the back first. Well, how would I know that?

When the sergeant seemed to be ready, the colonel stood to one side of it and ordered him to fire. Well, it was quite something! An incredibly loud noise, making the sergeant totter as it recoiled. It cut a swath through the bush, and its casing was ejected about four yards to the rear.

"Wow! Very impressive," Richard said. "Thank you very much for demonstrating that, and good luck up in the hills."

A few weeks later, the guys in camp were talking and said that when the army had gone up into the hills to get the stolen cattle back, they had walked into a trap. The Karamojong had surrounded the army, and they had lost many personnel. They were dug in, and were waiting for reinforcements.

"Yes," Richard said, "I thought the colonel had underestimated the Karamojong. We know that they see us out in the bush, but we don't see them. They'll be in their element up in the hills, and that's exactly why they are up there."

In all honesty, nothing much surprised me any more. Richard took life in his stride and I was happy to follow.

On occasion, when we returned from a capture in the Karamoja bush, covered in sweat and dust, we would drive down to Chepsikunya, the nearest village, and wash off at the village pump. The water felt so icy cold, it was almost a test of bravery to pour it over yourself! It was one hell of a contrast from the heat all around. I would brave it and I always felt great afterwards. The village kids were always great when they came around to watch us, and they thought we were hilarious – the best fun since our last visit.

As we moved through the seasons, from March through to May, you'd get what they called the short rains, bringing sudden downpours, with huge raindrops. The rain certainly settled the dust but it always left me feeling very cold and I would shiver all the way back to camp. The long rains would come later in the year, from September through to November.

The African thunderstorms were something else. On one occasion in Karamoja camp, a storm broke directly overhead, with the first clap of thunder coming totally out of the blue as I came downstairs from my room. I was really afraid; it was already dark, and the streaks of lightning were suddenly shooting across the sky, followed immediately by crashes of thunder. I froze on the stairs, not knowing what I should do – going back upstairs felt like a vulnerable place to go, but where wasn't? I decided to carry on downstairs and, just as I reached the bottom step, a huge streak of lightning seemed to shoot through camp. (I am convinced it was grounded by our camp entrance.) It was then followed by an incredible bang of thunder – I had never seen or heard anything like it. I had never in my life been afraid of thunder but that definitely set my heart a-thumping. Thankfully, the storm soon passed, but I will never forget how frightening that was.

Between capture sessions, we would check the animals and the stores, and keep abreast of camp life. It was my job to keep tabs on cash and cash flow to the camps, and on general safari expenses. I would sit with the camp managers (Ann in Karuma and Nell in Karamoja) and go over expenses and general outgoings, and I'd replenish their cash boxes when necessary. Staff too would often ask for an advance on their wages, although most would wait and collect their money in full at the end of the safari.

Occasionally, I would get to do different things when the Boss had gone back to England for a few days. If it wasn't checking out the Budongo sawmill way across country for the timber for making crates, it could be checking out the monkey and bird trappers up-country. I would sometimes have to go to Nairobi on a shopping trip when specific items were required, otherwise I could just take the time to chill out by the lake until his return. I liked to swim, or sometimes take a trip out on the water in the inflatable we had.

Richard would usually bring us back the odd item of clothing from the UK, mainly jeans, shirts or T-shirts, so if we had to go out to the bank or the hotel, it was nice to have something a bit more decent to wear. We normally just wore shorts and old shirts to keep the sun off us, but there was a decree from Idi that we should not wear shorts or have long hair. (You would think we'd have got one right!) We'd always toe the line when we were in town by wearing jeans and possibly a hat, but upcountry it was the usual bush attire.

These were harsh times in Uganda's history, and we were ordered out of Uganda many times for no reason other than being British, I think. During the evening our guys would listen to the radio and keep us up to date on such situations.

The simple solution for us, if there was any trouble, would be to hit the road north to Karuma. We also kept a 175cc motorcycle hidden behind a false back wall of our equipment store in Karamoja, just in case we were in danger or the army commandeered our vehicles. At least we could use the motorcycle to take the small mountain roads of Mount Elgon and drop down into Kenya.

When we were bush, though, we just ignored it but, on one occasion when Ann and I were in Entebbe, I felt I should check in with the British High Commission in Kampala. When we got there, we found ten to fifteen people carrying boxes and cases and goodness knows what else out of the offices; they were all in the process of leaving the country. We then decided we should make contact with the Swedish Consulate and discovered that the Swedish Consul was the manager of Grindlays Bank in Kampala and, would you believe it, he was English.

We arranged with him that in the case of an emergency, and if the current situation didn't blow over, we'd all leave under the Swedish flag. It did blow over, but we later gathered that poor old Hennessy, the British High Commissioner, had gone bowing and scraping, begging forgiveness for something we hadn't done so that Idi would allow us to stay.

We would try to go into Entebbe at least once a week and we'd use this time to draw cash from the bank in Entebbe, if we needed to replenish the funds (we didn't like carrying too much cash with us, but we couldn't afford to run out), and to collect the mail from the Lake Vic Hotel. It was always nice to get mail from home and, of course, we would write letters home too. As well as holding incoming mail for us, the Hotel would take our letters and post them home for us too. Virtually all mail arriving from outside of the country was censored, opened and read, prior to delivery. Sometimes mail didn't arrive at all, so we assumed it had just been confiscated.

On those weekly visits to Entebbe, we'd often take dinner at the Lake Vic Hotel too, just as a reminder that civilisation wasn't that far away, and Richard would also take the opportunity to make any phone calls he needed to. It also gave us a chance to wear our new clothes, which was something of a bonus, really. They sometimes showed movies at the hotel too, and I remember watching *Once Upon a Time in the West,* starring Charles Bronson. It was a great film, but the hooting and cheering once Bronson started gunning the baddies down was just something else!

Towards the end of my first capture safari, Richard left me in Karamoja to check the crates were completed and okay for animal transportation, while he went over to Karuma to do the same. Bruce Fenn had been flown out from the UK to build the animal crates at Karuma, while Peter, the Kenyan carpenter, had built the crates in Karamoja. Peter was from the Kikuyu tribe, the same as Kenya's then President, Jomo Kenyatta.

I'd always spend my free time in Karamoja out in the bush with Masabai, Patrick and Prospare. It really did feel like we were in the land of 'cowboys and Indians', except I was not thinking I could be scalped at any minute. We'd catch glimpses of people as we passed through the bush, and then they'd be gone. I would stop and reverse to try and see them, but I never did

Punctures were always a problem in the bush, so we always took a couple of spare wheels and a set of tyre levers with us. That way, if we ran out of spare wheels, the guys would remove the tyres, pack them with grass, and put them back on the vehicle. That would work well enough to get us home.

If we came across poachers while we were out in the bush, we had instructions from the Game Department to disarm them. Once, we encountered a very fierce Karamojong with brand new spears, and we stopped him and I asked if I could buy his spears from him. He was happy to give them up and, after a little bartering, I gave him a hefty two hundred shillings for them (£10). He was happy with that. We had disarmed a poacher as per instructions, and I now had prize possessions; a good job all round.

The poachers we'd come across were only hunting for food for their families, and were what I would term 'good poachers'. Nothing more than man has done throughout time. On several occasions at Karuma, though, we witnessed how ruthless the army could be, machine-gunning animals – even in the national parks – but there was no evidence of large-scale poaching by organised gangs for elephant tusks and rhino horns as there is today.

We generally worked seven days a week and it never crossed my mind that it could be any different. It was a way of life to never have a Monday morning feeling; every day seemed to be the same, yet completely different. Although I was often totally bushed at night when I hit my pillow, I never ever tired of the work and of what I was doing. I really loved it, plus I got paid for it. I considered myself a very privileged person and probably one of the happiest people on the planet.

Africa is a wondrous place, and every capture safari felt like a wonderful adventure.

Chapter 16

The Boss had gone over to Karuma to finalise the crate-building, and I stayed in Karamoja doing much the same as I usually did. Life was very laid back there, and it was good to spend time with the staff and the animals that we had caught. We went on the odd excursion to the bush, and I simply loved cruising the capture plains, viewing the animals but leaving them in peace.

I found it all so spectacular and thrilling to have the freedom to roam the bush. However, it was all about to come to an end as all the animals' licences had been filled. The next big adventure for me was to crate and transport the animals back to Europe.

Late one afternoon, after yet another wonderful day in Karamoja, a runner (someone you trust with a sum of money to reach a destination with a message for a particular person) came into camp with a message from the Boss, who was at the Lake Vic Hotel: "Call collect". So I set out with my companion Masabai, to drive some eighty kilometres to the Mount Elgon Hotel in Mbale, which was the nearest phone that I knew of.

When I got there, I wandered into the hotel and strolled over to the reception counter, and said I'd been told to call collect to my boss in Entebbe. I kind of knew it was a reverse charge call, but thought it better to ask and be sure. As I did so, I suddenly sensed someone close by my side. I glanced to my right, and a girl said, "Do you want to know what a collect call is?"

Well, she was quite something: dark-skinned, deep brown eyes, jet-black hair swept back, and the start of a smile crossing her lips.

"Yes, that's right," I managed to say.

"Well, it's a reverse charge call."

"Thank you," I said with a smile, and she then turned and walked away.

There was a phone cubicle along the wall to my left, so I asked the receptionist to make a reverse charge call to the Lake Vic Hotel in Entebbe, and told him the number.

I looked around and could see the girl sitting on a bench towards the end of the reception hall. When someone said, "Your call is at the cubicle, sir," I took the call. The Boss told me there was a ship leaving Mombasa for Plymouth in about a week's time, and told me I'd need to start moving animals down to Tororo train station, ready to be shipped down to Mombasa. He said he'd join me there.

So, I had a great deal of work to do. Abdu, an Arab gent who had a feed store where you could buy almost anything you can think of, was my best bet for help with my mission. I thought I'd call in to see him on my way back to camp and get him to organise some lorries for the transport.

I wandered down the corridor to where the girl was seated, and sat down beside her.

"Thank you for that," I said.

"No problem."

When I asked her if she was staying at the hotel, she said she was there with her father. He was away in Kampala on business, but was due back in two days' time, and then they'd be going on safari.

I offered to buy her a drink in the bar, as it seemed the least I could do.

"Yes, thank you," she said, standing up.

When we got to the bar, I asked her what she'd like to drink.

"Well, I think gin and tonic is the most appropriate drink out here, as the quinine in the tonic will help fight malaria should I be bitten by a mosquito carrying it," she said.

"Good thinking," I said.

We sat at a table and I called the barman over. I ordered her a G & T and a coke for myself. She asked me what I did in Uganda, so I told her

111

about the animal capture, and that we had a camp some fifty miles east of there.

"Wow!" she said. "That's interesting. What do you catch?"

I told her about the giraffe, hartebeest, roan antelope, eland, topi and ostrich we had at Karamoja, and about the elephant and buffalo we had at Karuma.

"It is the end of our capture now, and that phone call was to tell me a ship has been arranged to carry our animals from Mombasa to Plymouth in the UK," I told her.

Our drinks arrived and I found myself looking at the girl properly for the first time. She was very beautiful; those dark brown, near-black eyes were so captivating, her skin like tinted porcelain. A picture of this man's desire, for sure.

"Where is home for you?" I said.

"Our home is in Bergamo, close to Milano, north of Italia. It is very beautiful place," she said.

"We have been talking, but I don't know your name," I said. "I am Pete."

"Nice to meet you, Pete. I am called Nadia."

"Nice to meet you too, Nadia."

We both smiled and laughed. I asked her if the hotel was comfortable, as I'd been there occasionally but never stayed.

"Yes, it is very nice," Nadia said. "I could show you the room after we finish our drinks, if you wish, before you have to go."

And she did show me her room, from various angles and positions, for the best part of the next two hours. She really was beautiful and, thankfully, I was just what she wanted and appeared to desperately need.

Eventually, I told her I had to go as time was of the essence with an animal shipment to organise. I slinked away from the hotel, feeling like I had been through a mangle. When I reached the truck, I found my trusted friend Masabai sleeping across the front seats. As he roused himself, he asked, "*Je, kila kitu ni sowa bwana?*"

"Yes, everything is fine, thank you Masabai," I said.

How I really felt was drained, not fine.

It was too late to call on my Arab friend on the way home, but it did mean I could hit my own bed sooner. Early the next morning, my first priority was to get clean and then go to see Abdu to organise the lorries. As always, he was very obliging but he didn't have any lorries for me at that moment. That was a bitter blow, as it meant I'd need to start transporting the animals myself.

We had the staff to provide the muscle, but until our Bedford lorry returned from Karuma, I'd have to take the giraffe, one at a time, on a Humber truck. The crate just fitted within the sides of the truck, but we were really well-laden, as I took guys with me to help get the crate off at the station. We were quite a sight: the solid sides of the crate came just above the shoulder of the giraffe and, although there was a high surround to the crates, there was a very long neck sticking out of the top of it and plenty of acacia branches tied around it for the giraffe to feed on during the journey.

It was quite an ordeal – loading first, then driving the ninety kilometres-plus to the station in Tororo. I transported food too and, of course, I had to leave staff to attend to the animal's needs so I could go back and load another giraffe. On my way back to camp, I stopped off to ask Abdu if he had managed to organise any lorries yet, but the situation had still not improved.

To my great relief, the Bedford truck returned from Karuma just as I was setting out on my second train station run. That lifted the pressure somewhat as we could get four giraffe per load on that. When I returned to camp after that trip, Abdu had also sent two lorries, which really made a huge difference too.

I took one more trip to the station with a couple of topi, and was then able to check with the stationmaster that they had bogies (flat-bed carriages) that we could load the animals on to, and there was good news there too.

Richard arrived while I was at the station, having stopped off en route at the camp to see what progress we'd made. Once he too had checked things with the stationmaster, he said we should return to camp.

"Yes," I said. "Can we grab a cold drink in Mount Elgon Hotel on the way?"

"Yes, sure," he said. "That's unusual for you."

"Yes, I just feel in need," I told him.

As we took a drink in a shaded area at the front of the hotel, we discussed the shipment. Richard also told me that the next time we went to the station, I should take my belongings with me, as I may need to accompany the animals on both the train ride and the sea voyage.

"Okay," I said. "I would just like to check on something at the hotel desk first, if that's okay?"

"Yes, sure."

At that point, Nadia came out of the hotel with someone whom I assumed to be her father. They were obviously checking out of the hotel, judging by the baggage they were carrying. She glanced over in our direction, smiled, nodded and mouthed goodbye, with a broad smile. I smiled back and mouthed goodbye too. None of this went unnoticed, of course, and Richard asked me who that was.

"Just an Italian girl going on safari with her father, who's been in Kampala on business. She is a real free spirit."

"How do you know that?" he asked.

"Nadia and I went on a safari together last night! She took me on one hell of a journey. I'm still recovering."

He smiled, nodded, and said we should get back to camp.

When we got back to camp, it wasn't the neat, well-organised retreat we were used to – it was looking somewhat in disarray, due to the animal-loading. However, now that the last of the animals for this voyage were at the station, or at least en route, we could soon get things back to normal.

I needed to get my belongings together and get back to the station, ready to travel with the shipment at least down to Mombasa, if not further. My belongings had changed somewhat during my stay in Africa.

I had given most of what I had brought with me from home to the various guys who looked like they could use it. My kit had reduced from a large holdall down to a small bag, hand-luggage size, in which I had whittled my belongings down to the bare essentials: a couple of pairs of shorts, a couple of pairs of jeans, three shirts, socks, undies, handkerchiefs and my bandanas. Out there, I pretty much lived in shorts and bandanas. Before I left England, I'd had no idea of how things would be, or what exactly I'd need. The amount of unnecessary luggage I'd dragged around the world just in case it was needed, was amazing.

Chapter 17

Back at the railway station in Tororo, the bogies were shunted alongside the platform, and the guy got them loaded. There were twenty giraffe, five buffalo, five elephant, five eland, five topi and five hartebeest.

Prospare was to travel down with me, not only to see I got food and plenty of tea on the journey, but also to help with the animals. I sent him off to buy a primus stove, a kettle and a pan of his choice; we needed food, not a banquet. The catchers accompanied me too, by way of a bonus, really; they worked on the way down, and then spent a few days in Mombasa.

The whole thing was an incredible experience. The train, a steam locomotive, wound its way out of Uganda then up the escarpment; it travelled so slowly at times that I could walk alongside it for a while to stretch my legs. We created great excitement at each station we stopped at, with people rushing to see the giraffe, in particular.

The views were spectacular, overlooking the Rift Valley, and the simply incredible lakes of Nakuru and Navasha. There was a station stop, basically for water, as we crossed the equator. I found it all quite magnificent and to actually stand on the equator was very surreal.

My home for the three-day journey was less magnificent: a mattress under a sheet, which came down at an angle from the top of a giraffe crate. Home is where you hang your hat, they say, but in my case, it's wherever I throw my mattress.

Two guys from the UK joined us at Nairobi station for the rest of the journey down to Mombasa. They were both going to accompany the shipment by sea to Plymouth, which let me off the hook this time.

When we got to Mombasa, Richard took me to the Diani Beach Hotel, where I spent a couple of nights. This was total luxury to me. I swam in the Indian Ocean – it was just me on a deserted beach, bleached white sand, fabulous! I had my first knickerbocker glory and my first banana split ice creams in Mombasa (ice cream had only ever come in a tub or a cone at home, so this was all new to me), and I even had the odd beer.

I lived the high life there for a couple of days and nights (not all of the nights alone), before flying back to Entebbe. No mid-air panics this time; we flew on a small Fokker Friendship plane up to Nairobi then took the scheduled evening flight, on a DC9, to Entebbe. Ann met me at the airport; we took dinner at the Lake Vic Hotel, then stayed the night down at Nakiwogo.

The following day, we drove up to Karuma, as arranged with Richard, and I spent another couple of great days with Ann. By now, I could haggle at the roadside when purchasing banana leaves from the ladies in Karuma village, which obviously pleased them, but I didn't realise that this would be my last visit to Karuma.

When Richard returned, he had potential dates for the next sea trip from Mombasa to Plymouth. There was also a flight scheduled to carry fifteen elephant to Germany, but this was to take place after my departure.

Richard said we should go to Karamoja to finish up there. The next shipment was much the same as the first, but better organised this time with the full complement of Bedford truck and lorries from Abdu.

I once again went on that wonderful train journey but also accompanied the animals all the way to Plymouth. It was just me this time, though, and it was something of a shock after having got used to having so many guys around. I was very grateful when a junior officer onboard volunteered to help me – he was a hard-working guy, and relieved me of a great deal of pressure – but unfortunately, no sooner had we got on board, than we were off to sea. The sea breeze did very little to help me tie the remaining sheets down, plus, I was also starting to feel quite seasick.

Thankfully, the junior officer was happy to tend to the giraffe in their crates, as the ship had started to roll a great deal. In fact, if I stood at the side of a giraffe crate as the ship rolled, I could put a foot on the crate, grip the top rail, and ride up to the top of the crate. I used that opportunity to put food in the feed troughs and then, as the ship rolled back again, I just stepped off and back onto the deck.

My seasickness continued for around ten days; it was more just feeling sick than actually being sick, but not a nice situation anyway. The steward brought me a small concoction to drink, which burned all the way down but it did make me stand up straight and I didn't feel sick again.

There was only one real incident at sea. I saw some of the ship's crew speeding up to the front end of the ship, and discovered it was because the door to one of the buffalo crates, which slid up and down, had been knocked out of the runners when an over-enthusiastic breakfast-eating buffalo hit it. The animal hadn't tried to escape, it just carried on eating its breakfast. I took advantage of its attention being elsewhere to lift the door, drop it back into the runners and nail it into position. The what-ifs of it rushing around the ship didn't bear thinking about.

After a twenty-five-day sea voyage, I was relieved to get home and tread on dry land once again. I was also looking forward to seeing my family and friends, going to the safari park where it had all started for me, and having a pint of dark mild in the Magpie Bar.

Home! It was a real pleasure to be there but life felt a little different for me now, somehow. I'd left England as a sheltered 24-year-old 'country bumpkin', and now I felt hardened, fit and quite confident. I had learnt I could survive the most punishing of situations in one of the most dangerous countries at that time and I somehow felt I had come of age, matured. We all think we are Jack the Lad from the age of 16, but I only really grew up out in Africa. There was always so much potential for things to go wrong and, perhaps because of that, I'd found the experiences really thrilling. My time in Africa birthed in me a new awareness of how expansive and complex the world really was. It broadened my outlook and my horizons too.

I'd arrived home at the end of June 1974 and, on the 13th of August, Richard sent me back to our camp in Nakiwogo on the shores of Lake Victoria; he wanted me to organise a shipment of ten colobus monkeys and twelve crowned cranes back to England. In many ways, that short trip was almost like a break, as all of the paperwork went smoothly and everyone – from the airline's freight booking to the Game Department for export licenses, and the local vet who had to issue a health certificate – was helpful and efficient.

Richard joined me there for a couple of days too, which was very pleasant. Normally, life around Richard was very much about getting the job done but this time the job was already done. There was just one hiccup, though: the day before we left, a crowned crane damaged its leg and I felt we shouldn't send it back to England injured. However, as always, a resourceful team of guys came up with a plan: they lured some wild cranes into our camp, one of which made its way back to England the following day.

Back home again, I continued to work in the safari park and, in early October, Richard called and asked me to meet him in London, which of course I did. He was sending me back to Uganda once again. It filled me with great joy and excitement to be setting out on my second capture safari.

Chapter 18

October came around and Richard told me I was to fly to Kenya and collect vehicles from Ken Stewart's farm at Langata. I had met Ken on a couple of occasions when I'd been in Nairobi – once when Richard had introduced me to him, and then again when I'd been collecting items for Richard.

Ken was a Kenyan national and had his own animal capture business there. I gathered Richard had spent a great deal of time with Ken before setting up on his own in Uganda. Richard did that because he wasn't Kenyan-born, which you had to be at that time to acquire the required Grade A trapper's licence in Kenya.

"Pick up various supplies, Pete. Ken has a list of things that we will need. Once you have them, head on down to Uganda," Richard told me. "When you're there, go to the Game Department and see Ruaza. Tell him I am on my way, and ask him please to start organising capture licences."

He also told me to start setting up the camp in Karamoja. He gave me cash, mostly Kenya shillings, with some Uganda shillings, and told me I could collect more cash after I'd arrived in Uganda.

He also said Bill Diaper, a mechanic, would be going out with me and told me to meet him at Heathrow Airport. It would make a big difference to have a mechanic with us on safari.

"Okay, how will I recognise him?" I said.

"Oh, you can't really miss him," Richard said. "He's about five foot ten, very pale skin, black hair swept back and, when he smiles, you will see his canine teeth are somewhat longer than the rest of his teeth. I will tell him to wait by the check-in desk for you."

"Okay," I said. "Is it a night flight?"

"Well, they normally are," said Richard. "Why?"

"You just described Dracula," I said.

Thankfully, Richard found that amusing. He then told me Ann would meet us in Nairobi, and we'd all drive down together. Richard still had to decide whether he wanted to set up the elephant camp in Karuma again or maybe in Chambura. Both areas had large elephant populations but Ruaza had thought Chambura would be the better area because it had larger numbers of elephant there.

When I got to the airport, Bill wasn't yet at the check-in, so I waited there for him. I got a tap on the shoulder, and when I looked around, a guy I had met before but whose name I didn't and still don't remember said, "This is Bill, he will be flying out with you tonight, Pete."

"Okay," I said, and put my hand out to Bill as he approached. "Nice to meet you, Bill."

"Likewise," he said.

Perhaps it's best if I just say that Bill did fit Richard's description of him.

The guy who'd introduced me also had some insurance paperwork for me to sign in case of accidents. Just as well he knew me, or perhaps Richard had given Bill a description of me too? If he did, I wonder how he described me!

We flew on a scheduled flight this time, not a horrendous charter like last time. No panics, thunderstorms, or waitresses sprawling in the aisles. It was a very pleasant flight, and I was grateful for that.

Bill and I arrived in Nairobi and, when we booked into the Hilton Hotel, there was message from Ann to say she'd arrived and to let me know her room number. I called her once I'd settled in my room, and she came over. The three of us took lunch together and then went out to see Ken in Langata, in the suburbs of Nairobi, where our vehicles were stored.

When we got to Ken's place, there were two brand new Toyota Land Cruisers waiting for us, as well as the VW Kombi pick-up we'd had the previous year. Geoffrey Gibbon, a friend of the Chipperfield family for many years, had been out and organised the new vehicles but for some reason took the log-books back with him when he returned to the UK.

We collected all the goods we needed to take with us – some we got from Ken, and the remainder we shopped for. We stayed another night in Nairobi and set off the following morning for the Uganda border. It was always a fantastic drive, the scenery just something else; I always liked catching sight of Lake Nakuru and Lake Navasha, and picking out the large areas of pink where the flamingos congregated. Looking down across the Rift Valley was always spectacular too. I had done this trip a few times, when I'd gone to collect supplies and when I'd gone to deliver an elephant. It really was a wonderful trip.

There was a lot of talking at the border, mainly because Bill had no visa and we had no log-books for the new vehicles. However, we eventually managed to uphold what we jokingly called the 'company slogan': *B/S beats brains every time*. It was something we believed and, I have to say, relied on. It did help, although I think they recognised Ann and me from previous trips too.

Once we were over the border, the drive was pleasant but not quite as spectacular as it was on the Kenyan side. I was very familiar with the A109 road, as I had travelled it so many times with Richard. I was always very happy to be in Africa. It was a different world and I'm sure the sunshine, which I've always loved, helps a great deal with that happy feeling too.

I took care when driving through Jinja, as there was a large army barracks there, and then we continued on over the Victoria Nile via the Jinja Nile Bridge. The bridge is just before the Victoria Nile meets Lake Victoria, where it is said to start. Once through Kampala, we left the A109 and picked up the Entebbe road. I had spent the odd hour in Kampala but I'm a country boy so such places are fine for a visit but I am always happy when I am leaving them. London, Nairobi or Kampala – I feel the same about any major city, really.

After passing through the now familiar Entebbe, we were very happy to arrive at our camp at Nakiwogo in the late afternoon. The camp was in a beautiful spot, and the sun was going down rapidly to give us an exquisite sunset over the lake.

We hadn't warned anyone in camp that we were coming down, so they were surprised to see us. There was a little panic as to what they would feed us, but we said we'd go to the Lake Vic Hotel for dinner. When we got to the hotel, Lassie gave us a lovely, friendly greeting – he seemed genuinely pleased to see us.

It was a very pleasant but quiet evening, as not many people visited Uganda in those days. It was a great shame, really, as it is a beautiful country. I also felt a pang of sadness, knowing we wouldn't be seeing Paddy there either.

After dinner, we retreated to our little campsite and, as per usual, I was more than ready for bed, as were the others. We'd had a long drive – seven hundred kilometres (four hundred and thirty miles).

The following morning, after our breakfast porridge, I collected some cash and Ann and I went to the Game Department to see Ruaza. I explained that we were there to start setting things up for Richard, and that he would be arriving in a few days.

Ruaza hesitated at first and then said, "Please speak to Mr Chipperfield, and tell him that this year is not a good time to be in Uganda."

"Mmm, yes," I said. "I will call him and tell him what you have said."

These really were troubled times in this wonderful country, under the violent dictatorship of Idi Amin. I knew we should heed the words of someone such as Ruaza.

We left the Game Department and went straight to the hotel so I could call Richard and tell him what Ruaza had said. Richard said he'd get to Uganda as soon as possible and, sure enough, that evening we received a call at the Lake Vic Hotel to say Richard would arrive the following day.

We went to the airport the next evening to collect him and Terry Chivers, who worked at Knowsley Safari Park. Terry had been a keeper at London Zoo until he joined the safari parks, and he and I had worked together at Woburn when I was starting out too.

When we got back to Nakiwogo, we talked about our visit to the Game Department. Richard said he would go and see Ruaza first thing the next morning and talk to him. Richard did feel, however, that this could be a good time to venture into the Sudan. He'd spoken of us going to the southern Sudan during the last safari, so it was no great shock to hear that – we just hadn't expected to go this soon.

After he'd spoken to Ruaza the next day, Richard said we should pull back to Eldoret in Kenya and, once we'd all assembled there, then travel up to Sudan. Richard had originally wanted us to complete the Uganda safari first and then travel to Sudan to capture northern white rhino – a sub-species, then coming under pressure.

Ann drove Terry and Bill up to Karuma, where they collected the two Humber trucks, and then they travelled back down via Lira direct to Jinja, then Tororo, over the border at Malaba, and on up to Eldoret.

Richard and I went directly to Eldoret. We stayed at a hotel-cum-safari lodge establishment, which was clean and comfortable. There was a bar, so we went in for a coke, and saw a couple of guys playing snooker at the end of the bar room. After watching them for a few minutes, Richard said we'd be happy to play them for a couple of bob (shillings).

"Why not twenty?" one replied.

"Well, okay," Richard said.

When they had finished their game, they set the balls up again and said they were ready to take us on.

Thinking about it now I'm sure it seemed like a hustle, as Richard was very good at snooker, and I had also had a very misspent youth, playing virtually every day in the old working men's club in the village where I grew up. When it became obvious they needed to concede, both guys threw their cues across the table and walked out, without paying us our due. I was quite dismayed, but Richard smiled. Well, it was actually funny and we both had a good laugh about it.

The following day, the Bedford lorry arrived, as well as a Toyota HiAce, (a small lorry/pick-up), both well-laden with all the safari goods. Geoffrey arrived too and, when Ann, Terry and Bill joined us later that evening, that was all of us assembled.

It was good to eventually meet Geoffrey, as I'd heard quite a lot about him from Richard, and from colleagues back home who had worked with him in Spain. Geoffrey had also made the first contact with the Sudanese, when seeking permission for our capture of the rhino.

We were quite a convoy now, assembled behind the hotel, and Richard said we should split up; we didn't want to be of interest to the Ugandan army. It was quite a logistical operation, gathering a team and making sure we had the necessary papers to enter Sudan, and enough food and equipment for a few months in the bush. We also had to make sure our catchers, cooks and the rest of our guys had the right legal documentation to accompany us into the Sudan. They basically had free roam in East Africa but not in the Sudan.

We also had to carry fuel for our vehicles, and aviation-grade fuel for our light aircraft, which would arrive once we were established. We knew it would be different and difficult, and some of our African team were apprehensive about going into the Sudan at all. We knew what the situation in the Sudan was, but if there was coup in Uganda, anything could happen. So we took advantage of a lull in the fighting between North and South Sudan to enter the country.

Geoffrey, Ann and two Kenyan drivers were the first to set off from Eldoret. Their journey would take a little longer and would take them some six hundred kilometres over very poor roads: first the 82 to Kitale, then the A1 north, travelling around Uganda and up through Lokichogio to the border at Nakodok. They then had a further four hundred kilometres in the Sudan to the arranged meeting point at Likiberi, where we expected the roads to be even worse.

We set out the following day. I drove one of the Humber trucks, Terry followed in another Humber, Bill in a Toyota Land Cruiser, and Richard in a Range Rover. (He said he felt he needed a bit more comfort, which was fair enough – he was the Boss.) We headed to the Ugandan border at Malaba and, although we'd crossed that border often, we were always cautious. We were the same with any officialdom at that time, We'd always greet the officers with "hello" and a broad smile, working on the premise that happy people make others happy. All went well.

When the formalities were complete, we headed to Tororo, then Mbali, Soroti, and on to Lira. This route was familiar to me, as I'd driven it many times, when travelling between our camps at Karamoja and Karuma. I had with me my regular travel companions, Masabai, Patrick and Prospare, along with their personal belongings and some beds.

We were stopped by the police just after Soroti – it seemed they were suspicious of our convoy of vehicles. Richard had an excellent way with officialdom, which he'd honed over many years, and he managed to convince them we were just going about our business. It worked, and we were soon on our way again, on up through Lira towards the border. And that's when my accelerator spring broke and the pedal fell to the floor, on full revs.

As we often had to do in the bush, I improvised. I tied string around the pedal and up to the steering wheel, but this meant I had to drive with my foot hovering just above the accelerator, stretching the string to one side to bring the pedal up to the correct level to adjust my speed. It wasn't long before I lost power and we ground to a halt altogether – my fuel pump had packed up.

With Bill-mechanic's guidance, the guys dropped the fuel tank and then lashed it to the roof with strips of rubber inner-tube. We then ran plastic piping down to the carburettor to feed in the fuel by gravity. This worked, and we managed to continue to the border. I drove slowly, not wanting to attract too much attention.

Once the police and immigration officials were happy with our papers and passports, we cruised over to the customs post. Although the officers were officious, there were no problems but, just as I was about to move on, two army officers decided to check us out. Soldiers were always after money, especially Kenyan shillings for their buying power, so I'd always leave a little money for them to find. I never made it too obvious though, otherwise they'd look for more, and then I'd feign protest, saying I needed the money for the rest of my journey. I knew they'd take it anyway, and after they'd helped themselves to my 200 Kenyan shilling (£10), they waved me through and the other vehicles followed. We drove through no-man's-land to the Sudanese border, where the experience was far less daunting but the officials were thorough; it took a while for Richard and me to go through all the paperwork with them.

It would have been too risky for all of us to drive through Uganda, as the army could easily have confiscated our vehicles, as well as all our goods and equipment for the safari. We knew there'd be very little to buy north of the border, which was why we'd sent all the essentials with Geoff and Ann. We were thankful everything had gone well and we'd all made it safely through the border and into the Sudan.

Even though those worries were behind us, we had no idea what would be thrown at us in this country. Uganda had troubles of its own, but we were now entering a war zone; the North and South Sudan had been at war for many years.

Chapter 19

No-one pointed out to me that they drive on the right-hand side of the road in the Sudan, and there were no signs of any description anywhere. So we had a very nasty moment while driving on dirt roads (the tarmac had ended at the Ugandan border), when a heavily-laden lorry approached me in clouds of dust. Neither of us wanted to give way but, thankfully, he did at the last minute and took to the bush to avoid my vehicle. He managed, expertly, to keep control of his lorry; if he hadn't, we could have had a horrific accident. I felt dreadful when I realised what Masabai had been trying to tell me when he'd been babbling on at me.

My Humber sailed along nicely with the fuel tank still on the roof and the fuel still feeding into the carburettor by gravity. We did have a small pipe attached to the tank and if the engine started to splutter, one of the guys would blow into it, which forced the fuel through quicker.

The rest of the trip was uneventful but the dirt roads weren't great. They were a real contrast to the good Ugandan roads and the vehicles also stirred up so much dust that huge areas on either side of the road were covered in thick layers of it.

Apart from a few minor breakdowns, we drove non-stop through the night. Richard drove alongside me because my vehicle didn't have any working lights, but when a vehicle came the other way he would drop in behind me. I found it difficult to keep driving in a straight line, but my main priority was to avoid the bright lights coming towards me because, as I've mentioned before, no-one seemed to know about dip switches.

We were relieved to get to the meeting point and, having arrived first, I pulled over under some trees and our guys got our little camp organised. They boiled water for tea, lit a fire, and set up our beds, which were literally on the ground next to the road, with mosquito nets hanging from the trees.

Ann and Geoffrey and their co-travellers arrived just before dark, having completed one hell of a thousand kilometre journey over terrible roads. It was great we had all got to where we should be, safely and without incident, and the tea was very welcome as always. This time, however, it seemed extra special.

We spent the night under trees at the side of the road and woke up, ready for Sudan. Or so we thought. Richard and Geoffrey drove into Juba to the Game Department to collect all the licences for our activities; Geoffrey had negotiated with the Sudanese government on behalf of Richard, so everything was in hand – Richard just needed to collect the licences in person.

Back at our little encampment, I wandered down the road and couldn't believe how many ammunition cases I saw littered around the whole area. A little further on, at a small dried-up waterway, a little bridge had obviously been blown up and it looked like the scene of quite a battle. Everything was just so dry and barren, with no green in sight, apart from a tiny bit of grass that had found a drop of moisture from somewhere. Karamoja was quite dry but nothing like this, and Karuma was almost heavenly by comparison.

When Richard and Geoffrey got back, they said we should move to a better camping spot as it would be at least another day before their business in Juba was complete. So we packed up our beds, mosquito nets, pots and pans, and travelled about four miles down the road. This time we found quite a large, open, off-road area, with a number of substantial large trees offering relief from the heat. It was well over a hundred degrees Fahrenheit (about thirty-eight degrees Celsius).

After a second night of our gypsy-type life, we moved on to Juba and spent the night in the Juba Hotel. Great! We could have a complete wash and brush-up. The hotel was a really old, colonial-style hotel but the little comfort it afforded us was very welcome. We sat on the porch by the door of the hotel and drank some very dubious-looking orange cordial – the first cold drink we'd had for days – and it was very much appreciated. Bill and I shared a sparsely-furnished room, with two single beds, two uncomfortable looking round-backed wooden chairs with rattan seats, and two ceiling fans, one of which had an annoying squeak. It didn't really matter, though; we both managed to sleep very soundly.

For breakfast the following morning, we ate some fruit and a number of little finger-type bread rolls, which tasted like they had been made from millet flour, and of course drank several cups of tea. We then set out, heading north on the east side of the White Nile. The roads became very poor once we left the city, so travel was slow and there was the odd detour adding to the mileage, over rough roads to avoid bridges that had been blown up during the years of unrest. We were also obliged to check in at every police post en route to our destination. Often, that meant leaving the highway (I use the term lightly) to locate the police post in a village, and then returning to the main road once the paperwork for all goods and personnel had been recorded. We headed for Mongalla, which was just seventy-five kilometres away, but it took us close to two hours to reach there.

We spent quite a long time at the police station in the village of Mongalla, explaining that we would be setting up a camp close by, and going through all the paperwork with them. The point of interest for me, though, was the paddle steamers docked opposite the police station, which took people up and down the Nile, trading their wares. These paddle steamers were fantastic, like something out of an old film. It always fascinated me to think that all this would be going on, regardless of whether we were there or not – all the other people of the world going about their business that we never otherwise knew or heard about.

A friend of mine, Kit Thackeray, recalled a time he spent on the Nile. In his words:

Now the Nile isn't a straight river, and it's not always easy to see where the main channel is because enormous floating islands of papyrus move slowly up and down, pushed by current and wind.

The Master of the steamer Al Gutbi, a stern man with a silver beard, had developed his own technique for dealing with this set of phenomena. Based perhaps upon a passing liking for snooker, he would charge the flanks of these islands, hoping that this 'cushion' would bounce his unwieldy assemblage of craft roughly in the direction he desired. Often, the whole amalgamation would simply bury itself in thick vegetation, and this led to some surprising encounters.

The Dinka, southern Sudan's equivalent to the Masai and Fulani, are nomadic pastoralists, and they have taken to encamping on these islands for weeks at a time in order to get around Africa without the need to trek. When the prow of the Al Gutbi clove the greenery, and stopped just shy of their cooking area, it was seen by all as a great trading opportunity.

I was dressed, as usual, informally in my M and S underwear, a fetching leopard design which immediately took the fancy of a young, seven-foot tribesman. Dinka are tall men, and his height put him at an immediate physiological advantage over me at five foot ten. He inserted a finger into the waistband and pulled enthusiastically. When he let go, the elastic snapped back into place, which pleased him no end. Without further ado, he slid two ivory amulets down his arm and proffered them in exchange. I shook my head, and chose only one of them, worn and stained brown by sun, skin, cows and a few thousand miles of Africa.

So the deal was struck, and it was left to me to retreat to my cabin and remove the bartered goods. He suffered from no such sensitivity, and put them on right there on the deck.

"A little tight?" I ventured.

A stream of Dinka left me none the wiser, but he was pleased all right. He showed his friend. He thought it was a great deal, too. I just hoped any future lack of circulation would not affect him adversely after marriage.

At last, after many hours, the Al Gutbi and its barges managed to create an exit from the Dinka camp. Two cows were now mooing on the port barge, and I cannot imagine what was bartered for them. My brother, sadly no longer with us, had acquired a tasty looking cutlass, and although it was a handmade copy, the Dinka do possess all sorts of gear dating from the crusades, including chainmail, which they wear for their ceremonies.

From Mongalla, we travelled about fifteen kilometres further on, where we pulled off the road and down a small track to the Nile. We had permission to set up our camp on a large expanse of rough bushland to our left, and a large wooded area to our right. We built our camp within the wooded area as we felt that it wouldn't be obvious that we were there.

It really was a good spot, right on the Nile, and work started immediately. The guys set about clearing a large 40×40 yard area under the trees, and cutting back the foliage to make it a little safer for us. Keeping the foliage short meant snakes and the like would be less likely to try and make a home for themselves there.

Within about ten minutes of our arrival, the guys got the kitchen tent up, built a small fire, and made sure the tea supply was plentiful. We got to work erecting tents and unpacking our gear, and the guys put up tarpaulins, which they preferred to sleep under, nice and cosy in their camp beds. Once the all-important long-drop was dug, and the little bamboo shack put up around it, the camp began to look like home.

Richard and Geoffrey shared a tent as did Bill and Terry, and I shared with Ann. Déjà vu.

We soon started working on our main accommodation, which was to be an oblong building, running alongside the river. We built it ourselves using existing trees as uprights, lashing horizontal poles to the trees, using plastic sheet for a roof, with bamboo sheets on top and to the side up to window height, and mosquito netting around the top. We moved out of our tents and into it as soon as it was ready. It really was very comfortable and felt like home.

Mongalla was a very pleasant camp, with super shade for animals and humans. We also had the Nile as our very own private swimming pool right next to us, and it was quite special to be able to swim in it at the end of a dusty, hot day. Life in Africa: what more could you want?

On the downside, there were lots of snakes around. Our camp was in an area full of trees and thick undergrowth, which provided a perfect habitat for the snakes and, although we had cleared the area, it wasn't surprising some would slither back into our camp from time to time. Mostly, they would disappear into the undergrowth if we approached them, but on occasion we'd find them in our rooms, more by luck than anything else.

I shot two snakes during my time there. The first was on the day before Christmas, when a cobra reared up, ready to strike. Harming such critters was not what we did, or were there for, but this was just too close for comfort, and I felt I was in real danger. Fortunately, I had taken the .22 rifle with me, just in case of such dangers. My deed wasn't wasted, though – the guys ate the snake. It seemed they would eat snake whenever it was available, as I imagine it offered them a welcome change from chicken, which I'm sure they all kept at home and ate all the time. Snake meat wasn't something I wanted to try but the guys were so much closer to nature than we were. Even when I shot an animal for meat, they would always eat the internal organs too – they wasted nothing at all.

The second snake I shot was an unknown species, and I could see it trailing Ann as she swam in the Nile. It was definitely on a mission, so I decided to take it out – the last thing we needed was a snakebite emergency when we were so far away from any hospital or medics. Ann handled it very well, though, as a number of us – including local people – were shouting at her to get to the bank and get out. The snake was gaining on her fast and, the closer it got, the more difficult it would have been for me to shoot it and avoid hitting her.

Once we'd all moved into the long house and the tents were free, Richard despatched Ann and Terry to set up the rhino camp at Shambe. The rest of us set about building *bomas* to accommodate the various animals we'd be capturing: zebra, reedbuck and bushbuck. We built a large, round *boma*, which we padded heavily with grass thatch for the Mongalla gazelle, which are renowned for hitting walls and fences and losing their horns. There were literally thousands of Mongalla gazelle in the area, so they provided our protein as well.

When we had built what we considered to be enough *boma* space, we went out north of the camp for several miles and then went deeper into the bush to set out shark-netting for the capture of the gazelles. We strung a length of about a hundred and fifty yards of netting through the acacia bush, with the odd pole to keep it nicely upright, and tied helium-filled balloons to each end of it, making it visible to us so that we knew which direction to push the gazelle. Don't you just love it when a simple plan comes together?

On our first capture, we managed to catch two zebra and a reedbuck. On the way back to camp we spotted a ground hornbill, so we gave chase. You don't set out to capture such birds – it's something you do if you are lucky enough to come across them. They can only fly for short periods of time; because of their weight, their wings get tired. So to catch them, you drive towards them and they will take off and, as soon as they land, you need to be there again and probably again. By this point, they can only run because they're too tired to take to the air, and then it was all off the Jeep and run after them. Well, we all took part initially, but after the first twenty-five yards, Richard and I were just spectators. Afterwards, Richard said Patrick had run past him like he was standing still, and

Richard could really run too!

The land in the Sudan was very different from the capture plains of Karamoja; it was literally like driving over the ruts in a ploughed field. When we got back to camp, Richard told the guys to check every bolt in our vehicle to make sure they were still tight.

At camp, we had also cleared a nice wide area in the bush scrubland next to us for a landing strip for the light aircraft Richard had bought. It was a first for Richard to have a plane on a catching trip; he'd purchased the plane and employed Rory Falkner-Taylor – a Kenyan-born pilot, who lived in Nairobi and whom we came to call Rory the Pilot – for the duration of the safari.

We spent two full days working on every slight rise and dip until we were happy and felt it would be good enough to bring the plane in. The aircraft needed to be able to not only land but also to taxi to our camp entrance and turn around.

Geoffrey went to Juba Airport to wait for Rory to fly in and then flew back with him to camp and our landing strip. When the plane arrived, it circled overhead several times and flew just above the landing strip to check it out before attempting to land. He managed to land it all right, but Rory did end up getting a little more work done on the strip.

We also had a group of people join us from Dvur Kralove Zoo in the then Czechoslovakia: Jo Vagner, the Zoo Director, his son Zdenek, a keeper to work with the rhino so that he knew them when they got to their zoo, and three vets.

I had met Jo and Zdenek during the Ugandan safari the previous year. They had visited for a couple of weeks during the capture season, as we were capturing certain animals for them. They also travelled to Namibia (the then South West Africa), where they had animals on order. Jo used to mention a Murray-Watson (not sure of his first name), who probably did capture work for them there.

Jo and team had come to visit us in the Sudan, as the northern white rhino we were catching were for them. Jo had ordered the rhino for his park, and a number of other animals for his and various other parks behind the Iron Curtain. Although we were in the Sudan to capture the rhino primarily, we also wanted Mongalla gazelle for ourselves and possibly giant eland too. There were no Mongalla gazelles in captivity at that time, and there still aren't any now either.

Richard said we should attempt another catch in a different area, but it was really hard going. Jo went up with Rory the Pilot, with his camera, and they circled overhead, above us. We caught a reedbuck and then, whilst attempting to catch a zebra, we hit a warthog hole and an anthill simultaneously. In this truck, I didn't have the luxury of a nicely padded turret-hole for standing in; I had to rely on seatbelts, fixed at waist height across the top of the open cab, to hold me. However, when we hit the warthog hole and anthill, there was quite an impact and the belts couldn't hold me tightly enough; they stretched, and my chest hit the front of the truck, just above the windscreen. I flipped over the windscreen and ended up upside-down, hanging over it.

Richard pulled my legs down to get me the right way up and, once I unbuckled my belt, the pain sat me down on the seat where I had been standing. I felt sure something in my chest had actually moved on impact; I wasn't winded, but I needed to hold my breath until the pain subsided, which it started to do, a little.

Richard just said, "Are you okay?"

"I think so," I said.

"I can tell it's bloody painful because you've sat down," Richard said.

We then set off back to camp and, after a few minutes, I tried to look at my chest but it was just red. It was really painful to move, so I sat as still as possible all the way back.

Once back at camp, the guys offloaded the reedbuck and put it into a *boma* next to the one with the reedbuck from the previous catch. As I approached the *bomas* to check the animals, I noticed that the poles inside the *boma* that separated the animals hadn't been tied properly, so the animals had managed to get together and had started to fight. I felt I needed to do something, so I pushed through the pain and climbed up onto the roof to force a couple of poles apart so I could drop down inside and stop the animals fighting and injuring each other. I'd been resting on my arms and, when I dropped onto the floor of the *boma*, it felt like my chest literally pulled apart for a split second then snapped back as I hit the floor. For that split second, the pain was hideous but then it was gone; there was no pain at all as I hit the floor.

I grabbed both reedbuck by the horns, one in each hand to keep them apart, while the guys came to take them. The pain had just gone; I felt a little bruising if I touched my chest but, other than that, nothing. What I would have been like if I hadn't decided to separate the reedbuck I just don't know. It would seem the pulling and then snapping back in my chest placed everything back where it should be. It was a relief that that happened, because life just continued as usual from then onwards.

When Rory the Pilot saw me, though, he said, "I thought you were dead from that stopper; Jo thought so too, and I bet he has great photos."

Well, I was promised some but I never received any.

For the next couple of days, I went up with Rory the Pilot first thing in the morning, which helped me understand the geography and the landscape of the area. Flying around Africa – wow, I never thought I would be doing that. It was just wondrous, as we soared and circled with the vultures and Marabou storks in the beautiful, clear blue skies.

Richard, Geoffrey, Bill, and the Czech team then departed for Shambe to prepare for the next capture session. Rory also needed to get something checked on the plane in Juba, which could take a day or two. Wonderful, that gave me a little time alone and, a little like when we were in Karuma, some time in the evenings to catch up with the guys and to listen to their Maneno words. I loved hearing what they had to say. In general, they would talk about the day but none of the catching guys liked being in the Sudan, so their conversation was mostly about when they would get home.

I remember on one occasion listening to Koski, who was from the

Kipsigis tribe in Kenya and who had no front teeth, chatting to Muki, a Ugandan from the Baganda tribe, who had scars all over his face.

"What are all these markings you have all over your face, Muki? Are they supposed to make you look pretty? I can't imagine someone doing all that to my face," said Koski.

"Well," said Muki, "these cuts and marks were done when I was a baby and there really wasn't much I could do about it. You laugh at me but you were fifteen years old when someone knocked your two front teeth out. You just stood there and let them do it."

I half expected them to start fighting, but it was all taken in good humour and there was a great deal of laughter all round.

Chapter 20

When Rory the Pilot got back from Juba, he and I flew up to Shambe to join the others for the rhino capture. We set off down our little runway and were airborne very quickly, at only about forty to forty-five miles an hour, and we were going to fly along the White Nile, as the Shambe camp was to be built on the Nile too.

It was a great little trainer plane, with dual controls. Trainer, well I just had to have a go! I sat behind Rory, and the joystick was actually under my seat, so I extracted it and put it in position in front of me. Rory then explained a few things to me about air speed, flaps and throttle, which was on the left-hand side of the plane just below the window level. I wasn't going to actually fly the thing, just endeavour to keep it in a straight line and level with the horizon. I was a bit up and down at first, but I soon got the hang of it and it was fun, although keeping it level took so much concentration. I asked Rory to take it back, as the scenery and views and animals were simply too amazing to miss.

Rory was happy to drop quite low – about five hundred feet – to show me the best of it. We flew over swampland, where there were large numbers of elephant – huge, massive bulls with such massive tusks; they didn't take too kindly to our intrusion though, flinging their trunks towards us, ears out and some trumpeting above the engine noise, before heading off away from us. We saw large herds of buffalo and, again, there were huge, solitary bulls. No doubt these areas were quite inaccessible, too difficult for hunters to get to, and the war will also have kept such people away too. The food will have been good in this area too – with so much water around, the vegetation was really good. After the initial shock of seeing our little plane overhead, the buffalo too headed off. I can't imagine they saw many planes or humans.

Rory told me the tale of his arrival, when Geoffrey had gone to meet him at Juba Airport to show him the way to the camp at Mongalla. He said Geoff put on a leather flying hat and goggles, reminding him of Biggles (a fictional pilot and adventurer, hero of the W E Johns series of *Biggles* books). He then talked about getting to the camp.

"We were circling camp, when there was a sudden loss of power. I had no idea what had happened, but thought, where the hell is that landing strip? I frantically looked around, and then I saw the throttle had been pushed forward, cutting the revs to the engine. I quickly powered it up again and realised what had happened. Obviously, Geoff had been looking around and had put his hand on the throttle, inadvertently pushing it forward as he lent forward. It was a nasty few minutes," Rory said.

Rory and I got to the Shambe camp a lot sooner than I expected and were circling, making a couple of flights along the runway to check it out prior to dropping in and landing. It was a bit bumpy, but if you're not thinking about dying, it's quite fun! Flying was no real problem for me anymore.

So this is Shambe, I thought. Ann and Terry and team had done a lot of work getting the camp together. It looked good, if a little hot. The first thing I thought was, where's the shade? Although I was never really bothered by the heat, it was noticeably hotter here than in Uganda. They say mad dogs and Englishman go out in the midday sun, and I've always been a true Englishman.

It was good to catch up with everyone at camp. When I asked where I was sleeping. Terry said I was in with him, in the tent on the far left. I had a little wander around the camp, looked in at the rhino *bomas*, and Ann joined me.

"Best I could find," she said. "The only bit of shade in the area, those two big trees."

The camp was chokka, with twenty-eight of us, including the local team. That evening the Czechs all sat and ate together – it was a language thing, really, because only Jo and his son Zdenek spoke a little English and none of the rest of us spoke Czech, German or Russian, which they all did.

After dinner, Richard, Geoff, Terry, Bill, Ann and I sat chatting for a while but the mosquitoes were noticeably worse here too. After a while, we all started to drift off to bed, and I was one of the first to go. After a spray round of insect repellent in the tent and getting my mosquito net well tucked in, I was off. We needed a good night's sleep, as the following day we intended catching our first rhino.

After the morning cuppa, which this time didn't arrive at the bedside (not sure why, maybe there weren't enough cups to do that), Richard said I should go up in the plane with Rory the Pilot, to see if we could locate rhino. So that's what we did. It was quite amazing how quickly we were airborne and way up in the sky, and we found rhino very quickly. It was a perfect find, in fact: we found a mother and calf about the right age and, not much further on, yet another – also with a capture-size calf.

When we returned to camp, there was a great deal of activity preparing to go bush to capture the rhino we'd located. I would normally be gathering my gear together for roping the animals, but this time Richard's plan was to dart the animals rather than catch them with a rope. He'd managed to carry the tranquillising drugs in his suitcase from the UK: yellow M99 in an aftershave bottle, and the blue M50-50 antidote as cologne. Thank goodness the customs officer didn't check it and dab a little behind his ears. Atorphine (M99) is over a thousand times more potent than morphine and penetrates the skin easily. Needless to say, we too had to be ultra-careful during its use, as there was no medical expertise available should we have had an accident or spilt any onto our skin. A wet needle is enough to kill, as a number of vets had discovered to their cost.

Steven, who had met me at the airport along with Richard when I first arrived in Uganda, went up with Rory the Pilot as another good pair of eyes.

We then set off in our vehicle in the general direction of the rhino Rory and I had seen earlier, and soon Rory flew over us and guided us to the spot, with the aid of a two-way radio. When we were within stalking distance, we stopped and waited while Richard and Geoffrey went forward and loaded the dart with the M99. Once ready, Richard went a little nearer to within darting range, while we all stood silently waiting for the crack of the rifle as it sent the dart to its mark. There it was and, almost immediately, Richard returned but without Geoffrey. Richard sent me off to see where Geoffrey was, while he spoke with Rory over the radio to find out if he could see him.

As I moved forward, I spotted a large tree, which I felt could be very handy as even the rhino would have to go around that. I then heard the sound of feet running, and saw Geoffrey going flat-out with the rhino keeping up with him nicely. After they had disappeared from sight, I waited a minute or so and then saw Geoffrey walking back. Thankfully, he had managed to lose the rhino somewhere and looked happy to be on his way back without it. I have to say, he did look pale and he was very breathless too. How he got into that situation, I just can't imagine. He didn't ever offer an explanation either.

From the air, Rory spotted the rhino standing quite still next to an acacia bush, and kept watch on it while he circled, the Marabou storks and vultures overhead too. When we saw that the rhino hadn't moved for some time, we moved in. We were slow and quiet, but the animal was far from tranquillised and took off again.

Richard then decided to make up another dart and again went forward with the tranquillising rifle. Again, we played the waiting game, while Rory kept us informed about the rhino from the air. We soon realised that our problem was the dart needle. As the dart struck the rhino and the needle entered the animal's muscle, it will have 'cored'; that means that the hole in the needle would have become blocked with skin and fat as it entered, so when the dart detonated, it wouldn't have been able to push the drug into the animal. There will have been a certain amount of leakage, allowing a little to get through, but not enough to drop the animal to the ground. The second dart had had the same result, but the two small amounts of drug that got through were enough to enable us to physically restrain the animal and get it crated.

We were all exhausted and dehydrated after that capture outing, and it was a relief when we eventually got the animal back to camp. Days like we had just endured were unfortunate, but we would always have to see them through. It was a long, hard day all round for animal and humans alike, and what we had started, we had to finish for the animal's sake; that was the unwritten rule. And the day wasn't done yet – we still had to get the animal into a *boma* and make sure he was nicely settled before we could refresh ourselves.

Would you believe, the rhino had not just lain down in the crate but it was completely flat-out! Despite having been given the antidote to the drug, it refused to wake up, so eventually we had to manhandle it into a *boma*. As you can imagine, the rhino filled the crate, so it was difficult to get around it to move it; we applied ropes to the leg we could reach, but it took a good hour to be able to slide it from the crate and position it in the *boma*.

I have to say, I was totally shattered but I certainly wasn't the only one. We all needed water but it was in very short supply because of the demand. Eventually, I took it straight from the kettle, leaving it to cool a little but drinking it as hot as a cup of tea. Well, it was water and that is what I very much needed. I drank a couple of kettles-full of hot water that night; it wasn't as refreshing as lovely ice-cold water, but it slowly rehydrated me.

I didn't feel much like food; I picked about at my corned beef fritter but decided to call it a day. I went to bed just as I was – my hands were clean, but that was about it. I just collapsed on my bed and didn't move till morning.

When I got up, I discovered that despite being under my mosquito net,

I had obviously been lying against it and the mosquitoes had managed to bite me through it. I had multiple bites to my arms and legs, which were now itching like mad. I wandered down to see the rhino. Ann was already there and we were relieved to see the animal standing up. It was still quite groggy, and would need a bit more time to come round fully.

Back up by the tents, I took a bucket of Nile water around the back and had something of a wash, which refreshed me, if nothing else.

There was porridge for breakfast when I returned, which I enjoyed with golden syrup, no jam! There was discussion going on about the day's capture ahead, and Richard again wanted to tranquillise the rhino rather than rope it. I didn't think it would work and worried that we'd have the same problem as we'd had the day before. I think they thought I just wanted to rope the rhino, and perhaps they were right.

Very much like we'd done the day before, we set out again after Rory and Steven had been up first to spot the rhino from the air. This time, the animal took the first dart but refused to lie down. In frustration and, I think, a little exasperation, Richard suddenly said, "Pete, get your rope."

I almost shouted, "Yahoo!" but it didn't feel appropriate. I put my rope and pole together quickly. Richard took the driving seat in the Toyota and, with four guys on the back and my rope anchored to the truck, we were off. As with the animal the day before, this one was on the move as soon as it heard us coming. Drugged or not, they do love heading for the thickest acacia bushes around and it was a real struggle to avoid getting my rope entangled in the acacia. One of the guys on the back helped me and, as soon as we hit a small clearing, I dropped my rope over the animal's head and pulled tight.

Richard slowed the animal to a stop, and the guys were off. I did all I could to keep the rope tight so the guys could get around the animal and, with the aid of leg-ropes, they soon dropped the animal to the ground. Leg-ropes are short sections of rope, about six foot long with a noose on each end, which you put around the animal's legs, basically to hobble it and force it to drop to the ground. Once the animal is down with a cover

over its head, it is much safer for everyone all round.

We soon had a box there and, with a rope through the crate, the rhino was slowly allowed to stand and was pushed into the crate. The crate was loaded by the usual method of raising it up on tyres and then sliding it onto the truck.

Richard asked Rory to try and locate another rhino, which he did after about twenty minutes, so we loaded up and went after our third animal. The rhino mother and youngster were not so quick off the mark as we approached – I have no idea why – but they soon picked up the message and were off into the thickest stands of acacia around. Again, my biggest problem was keeping my rope and pole out of trouble. I had learned to keep the pole mostly at the back of the vehicle and not at the front, easier to manage in the acacia that way, but I had to be really quick bringing it forward to do the roping. Again, the guys on the back managed not only to keep their balance but also to help me a great deal with pushing the pole forward at the appropriate time. I roped the youngster, with Richard again bringing it to a stop and the guys doing their stuff with as much help from me as I could manage.

Once all was loaded, we set out back to camp. This time, I managed to take in my surroundings on the ride back. This landscape was different from what we were used to but it was still very much Africa. Fish eagles were of great interest to me and there were so many of them – I imagine the Nile gave them very good pickings.

We were back at camp in good time this time, with everyone obviously much happier and less exhausted than the day before. I know I certainly was.

The rhino offloading was far more straightforward than the previous day. A great deal of snorting and grunting from the rhino, as well as the odd charge at us while we got them secure, but we were soon able to leave them to settle down. The fact that there were other rhino around will have helped settle them too, I'm sure. The rhino we'd captured the day before was now quite with-it and also capable of some grunting, snorting and charging. That made us happy; what more could we wish for?

Our work done, I got myself clean – a couple of buckets of Nile water did the trick again but wow, the water was bloody cold! It was a bit like the pump-wash I'd had in Chepsikunya in Uganda, but without all the kids laughing at me and having fun.

We had a leisurely dinner and Richard said we should start back to Mongalla the following day, as he and Geoffrey needed to go to Nairobi.

Richard and Geoff set off first thing the following morning, while Bill and the Czech team all stayed on in Shambe. I flew back down to Mongalla with Rory the Pilot, with little detours on the way as I was so amazed by the swamp elephant and buffalo. I couldn't get enough of watching them. The wet swamplands were enormous, almost like very large lakes. We all but flew with a fish eagle for a little while – they really are magnificent birds.

When we got back to Mongalla, it felt a bit like coming home. I liked the camp, not as much as I liked Karamoja or Karuma, but it was certainly a comfort to see it again.

Chapter 21

A few days before Christmas, Richard and Geoffrey went to Nairobi again, most of the gang stayed on in Shambe, and Rory took the opportunity to go to Juba to check the plane out. On Christmas Eve, I shot a guinea fowl, which would be our Christmas lunch, and it was also the day I had to shoot the cobra, which the guys then ate.

The day after Boxing Day, I took some of the guys out and we caught a couple of gazelle. The following day we went out again to collect one or two more, however, in the process of driving them towards the net, I obviously cornered too sharply and felt the truck slide a little. I tried to control it but couldn't hold it and we rolled, ending up upside-down. I quickly checked and, apart from being upside-down and in a heap, I was okay.

I called out to the guys to see if they were all okay but all was quiet. My main concern was that I could smell petrol, and I was trapped; I couldn't open the doors. Then suddenly the truck shook, my driver's door was ripped open, and a hand came in, grabbing the collar of my leather jacket and dragging me out.

"Thank you, Patrick!" I said.

It wasn't a pretty sight. Josef had hurt his legs below the knee, and Simba had pain in his thigh. We got everyone up and, between us, we got the truck back into an upright position. We had two punctures, so we used the spare we had brought with us and packed the other with grass to see us home. We drained the oil from the air filter and poured it back into the sump. Then, just as we were ready to set out for camp, a number of people came wandering over towards us.

As they drew near, we could see they had had problems, as there was a great deal of blood on show. We learnt that the previous night there had been a fight in their village (not sure if it had been between the villagers or a group from outside) and most of these guys had been hacked with *pangas* – the five men and the two women all had huge gashes on their arms, legs and backs. It was quite horrific. They asked if we would give them a ride, which of course we did. We limped back to camp in our bashed-up truck, and I thought I'd take them all to hospital in another vehicle, but when I arrived Rory was there and kindly volunteered to take them all, including Simba and Josef.

Thankfully, our guys were only bruised and they recovered quickly. I was grateful for that, as I felt very bad about rolling the truck. I don't know if we rolled because we had two punctures, or it was just down to my bad driving, but either way it wasn't good.

The following day around mid-morning, when I was looking around the few animals that we had in camp, I looked up and there was Richard; I was surprised as he hadn't been due back for at least another day.

"Are you okay?" he said.

"Yes, physically anyway," I said. "I just feel such an idiot for rolling the truck."

"Ah, how is the truck?"

"Well, some of the guys have taken hammer and crowbar to it so it's a little straighter than it was."

I asked Richard where Geoffrey was, and he said he'd left him in Nairobi.

"I went back home for Christmas and, as I got off the plane in Nairobi, I told Geoff you'd had an accident. and I had to get a flight to Juba and a taxi out here to see if you were okay."

"Amazing," I said, "and thank you."

Richard and I did have a real connection. We had spent a great deal of time together but no more, I'm sure, than others doing my job before me had. When you work side by side, day in and day out, in many ways you do grow alike, think the same things, come out with the same statements at the same time, and so on. But this was different. There was definitely a connection. And this kind of thing had happened a number of times before, where I would send messages telepathically and Richard would receive them, but never before on this scale. Obviously I thought he'd been in Nairobi over Christmas, so that is where I sent the message telepathically, and that's why he picked it up as he arrived there. People often don't believe it happens; they'll just put it down to coincidence or imagination, but I've really experienced it. I am not just a sender; since the age of five, I have picked up other important messages too, which have quite possibly saved my life.

I went through the whole accident saga with Richard, telling him who had been injured and how they were now on the mend, and I also told him Rory had taken the villagers to hospital.

When Geoffrey arrived back the following day, Richard said, "Look what Pete's done to your truck, Geoff!"

"Yes," he said, "I'm glad I'm not the only one to have rolled a Toyota Land Cruiser!"

I thought that was very nice of him. Later I asked Geoff about Richard getting the message that I'd had an accident when he got off the plane in Nairobi.

"Yes, it was quite incredible," Geoff said. "He never said hello, no greeting at all, just 'Pete's had an accident.'"

That evening, Simba, Josef and Steven came around, saying they were getting head pain and not feeling so well. They said their injuries from the truck accident were becoming infected. Geoffrey said he would give them treatment and started by giving them two aspirin each. He then picked up a bottle of penicillin and a syringe and, whilst he drew the first dose, told them all to drop their shorts. Well, I have seen much kinder injections given to horses, I have to say, but he was dealing with men here. The first two took their injections with very pained expressions, although I'm not sure if they were just biting their lips or tongues to distract themselves. Steven called out the whole time Geoffrey was injecting the penicillin into his rump muscle.

"*Mziiiiiiiito! Mzito!*" (Pain).

They thanked Geoff (*asante*), and wandered off. They never came back complaining that the penicillin hadn't worked, so it must have done the trick, or else the treatment was worse than the infection.

On a previous safari, when a vehicle broke down and the guys were all hanging around, Geoff threw a rope over a branch. He tied a noose on one end and gave the guys a challenge: "Who thinks they can put this noose around the back of their head and pull themselves up until their head touches the branch?"

There were plenty of takers. First guy up slowly pulled on the rope and gradually reached the top, to big cheers.

"*Vizuri!*" (well done), said Geoff. "Now come back down."

Pulling up requires a strength that most guys seemed to have, but it's a different story altogether getting your muscles to work in reverse, lowering yourself back down, You face two choices, really – either stay up there or simply drop. The guy didn't know what to do, so the rest of the guys grabbed the rope and lowered him back down.

It is much like I found when I was trying to hold a giraffe's feet on the ground once we'd caught it. I could pull up and lift relatively easily, but I struggled pushing down to keep the animal's feet on the ground, until I too built the right power in my muscles.

The following morning, Richard sent me to collect his father from Juba and bring him back to Mongalla. Jimmy Chipperfield, of course, was *bwana mkubwa* (the big boss), who we referred to as Mr Jim. After his visit, I took him back to the Juba Hotel and, when I got back to camp, discovered we were having a Presidential visit.

We always kept champagne in the camp for just such a special occasion, but because the President was Muslim, he didn't drink. Between him and his entourage, they drank all of our water. We were very unimpressed.

A guy from the Game Department, who was with us the whole time, had been a colonel in the army and at that rank had always ridden in the front seat of a vehicle. It took a week, but we eventually managed to persuade him that we needed that seat for me; I always stood on the passenger seat to catch. He did get the message. And because I wore a gun whenever we went bush, he did too. But I'm left-handed, so wearing a right-hand holster, it always looked like my gun was the wrong way round. He took a couple of days' leave and, when he returned, he was wearing his gun on the right in a left-hand holster. I think that was the main reason he'd taken a break, to acquire a different holster. He obviously wanted to copy me.

When Richard and co departed for Shambe, Richard told me an American – Brian Vidor – was arriving a bit later too, so he told me to collect him from Juba Airport at 10am.

"I imagine he will be the only passenger getting off the plane from Nairobi, so you should find him okay," said Richard. "Then make your way up to Shambe, and we will go out for more rhino from there."

I collected Brian from the airport in Juba and we went straight on to Shambe, as opposed to going back to camp first, which would have added around a hundred and fifty kilometres to our journey. Brian had come out to see what went on and also to help out with the safari. He worked at a safari park adjacent to and part of Great Adventure Theme Park in New Jersey, which was run by a friend of Richard's called Butch Dring. Brian and I seemed to get on well right from the start.

The journey to Shambe was a long four hundred kilometres, over terrible roads and across bridges made from poles across waterways. It was all character-building stuff, as they say, and we certainly knew each other a lot better by the end of our six-and-a-half-hour trip. We got to camp just before dark. Food was very welcome and, although we'd had water with us for fluid intake, the tea was delicious.

The next morning, we were up early getting organised for the rhino catch. Rory the Pilot set off with Steven to locate suitable animals for capture and, while we were waiting for Rory's return, I wandered down to the rhino *bomas* with Ann. I was pleased to see the rhino were doing well and were amazingly well settled. They looked like they were in really good health and seemed at ease in their captivity.

As soon as Rory returned, we climbed aboard the truck and set off and, a few minutes later, Rory was up again, leading the way. When we stopped while Richard communicated with the plane, I checked out my equipment to make sure all was as it should be.

We then cruised through the bush with Rory talking us in and, when we had the animals in sight, we moved in. The mum and her youngster were soon up and heading for the thick acacia but, between me and the guy behind me, we managed my rope and pole very well. It wasn't easy, as we were ducking and weaving to avoid getting ripped apart by the cruel, unforgiving acacia.

It seemed an age until we got to a suitable capture area but as soon as we did, I roped the youngster and Richard slowed it to a stop. The guys were again off the truck with the leg-ropes and quickly laid the animal down. Again, it took a while for the box-wagon to find us, as we had gone quite a distance through thick bush. The rhino-loading worked like clockwork and, as always, the sheer power of our catching guys was awesome.

Once the animal was loaded, we had to just sit and wait while Rory scanned the area for another candidate. My leather jacket had saved me from the brunt of damage the thorn bushes could have inflicted, but it was impossible to avoid every thorn. (I clearly hadn't; twenty-five years later, some thorns started surfacing on top of my head. They appeared as pimples at first and then once they'd pointed, I was able to extract the thorn tips. I've found five so far, but who knows how many entered the body never to be seen again?)

We were soon off again, following the direction of the plane leading us in to where the rhino were. Once the animal was spotted, there was no time for discussion – not that it was necessary, anyway, as we all knew what we were doing and the chase was on. This time, it really wasn't a long chase but when you're pushing through the acacia with your head bowed, trying to keep it below windscreen level and taking scrapes to the hand holding the pole, it seemed like an age. Then, as before: the small clearing, the acceleration, very quick pole work, and we had another young rhino on the end of my rope. The second rhino loaded, Richard said that was enough for the day, and we returned to camp.

I spent time with Ann that afternoon, chatting and looking at and talking about rhino. Ann had created another well-organised camp here, which was testament to her total commitment. She was very much at one with Africa. Terry was a great asset to the rhino camp too.

The Sudan was hard on us all as life was difficult; whether it was collecting water, ensuring there were enough supplies, caring for the animals, coming across blown-up bridges, checking in at police posts, even general life in Sudan wasn't easy. The best of our camps were our sanctuary from what seemed all the madness of rules and regulations in the outside world.

Although the police wanted us to check in at the station every time we came in or out, we did manage to reach an agreement with the local police that when we were catching in the Mongalla area, we didn't need to check in at the station every time we went out or came in. On one occasion, after we had been out on a catch, I needed to go to Juba so I went straight on from the catching area as it would be quicker to do that. However, I checked in at the police station on my return and was promptly arrested and jailed for not going through the process on the way out. Well, strictly speaking, I *was* wrong but I didn't feel it was that serious. My main problem, though, was that one of the officers was so drunk he could barely stand, and I wasn't too sure about the other officer either.

So, with the aid of Masabai chatting to me through the cell bars, we made a huge fuss about the vehicle being left unguarded, which meant that there'd need to be an inventory made of all the goods and equipment, meaning the police officer in charge would need to sign the inventory and, in the event of any goods or equipment going missing, he would have to be held responsible. Should such a case arise, then the list would have to be handed to the Chief of the Game Department in Juba, who we'd been working in close co-operation with. After some deliberation, they released me and asked me to please go through the proper process in future. I agreed.

Masabai and I drove back to camp, laughing all the way back at our achievement. I was relieved too, as my cell was rather grim to say the least and I didn't fancy spending a night or more there. I'm sure Masabai will have related the tale to the rest of the gang when he got back in camp, for a bit of fun.

After we'd caught the two rhino, Richard decided we should head off to Mongalla to capture a few more gazelle and then take stock of the situation again. It was never good to be capturing day after day in the same area.

We drove back to Mongalla the next day, with Richard, Geoffrey and Bill travelling together, and Brian and Masabai coming with me. It was a long, dusty journey but very interesting; our camps were on either side of the Nile, so basically we travelled down one side of the White Nile and up the other to get to Mongalla.

All in all, I was happier at the Mongalla camp. It had somehow become my camp, and I was certainly more content there. Also, Zapiel made the most wonderful bread, which must have influenced how I felt too.

That night, as we were preparing to go to bed in the long building, Geoffrey mentioned the fact that when Richard arrived in Nairobi, he knew I'd had an accident, without being told. Bill and Brian were very sceptical about it and, after the conversation had gone on for a while, Bill said, "If you can do such things, why doesn't Pete send you a message right now?"

Richard wasn't keen but then agreed we should give it a try. I thought it may or may not work; in general, things that have been set up like that tend not to work.

"Okay," I said. "I'll send you a message."

There was some general chat, then Bill said, "You should have a message from Pete by now, Richard."

After a pause, Richard said, "Pete's thinking about the revolver." (A .38 Smith & Wesson which went everywhere with me.)

I said it wasn't the revolver, which generated quite a bit of mocking from Bill. In conversation with Geoff a little later, Richard said it was difficult being asked at random what someone might be thinking, because you try and think too much about what that person could possibly be thinking of.

"As silly as it sounds, the only thing that was in my mind the whole time was a huge bottle turning over and over, but then I thought, why would Pete be thinking of a bottle?" said Richard.

"Yes, why indeed," I said. "But that's exactly what I was thinking about. That magnum of champagne we have in the kitchen tent, just in case someone important should come to camp. That's what I was thinking about."

There was then some grumbling from Bill but he did become quiet on the subject after that. That connection with Richard was as strong as ever.

We were up early again the next morning and out to the capture site. On the way, we passed a Dinka camp (the largest tribe in the Sudan), where they had a lot of horned cattle. Most of the people were covered in white ash as they tended to sleep in the ashes of their day-time fires, which helped to keep them warm through the night. The Dinka are very tall people, I believe they are the tallest people in the world, with some having been known to reach seven foot ten inches tall.

Richard was driving and I was on the catcher's seat – it was just fabulous cruising the bush and I always loved standing in my catching position. Not that I was needed for the capture, as Richard drove the gazelle straight towards the net, zigzagging through the bush. I loved it.

We collected four gazelle to add to our collection, but a little oribi antelope had also got caught in the net, so we set it free. A bushbuck had got quite entangled in the net too, so Geoffrey went forward to free it. It leapt as he approached, knocking him down and rolling over the top of him, and we now had one bushbuck and one human in the net. It was quite amusing but also quite a dangerous situation for Geoff.

It was going to be very difficult to get them both out, so Richard said we should just cut the net as basically we'd finished with it. But even that wasn't easy. We managed to free Geoffrey first but we all had to pitch in and hold the bushbuck so we could cut it free. Our guys were a little upset that we didn't just take a knife to its throat and be done with it, as that would have kept us in meat for quite a while, but Richard said we should let it go.

When we got back to camp, I dropped into the Nile and spent quite a while just swimming up and down. After Ann's experience with the snake, I didn't like going out too far. We always carried snake stones with us in case we were bitten, and tended to carry them, along with a scalpel blade, in little leather pouches we wore around our necks. If you got bitten, you'd have to make a cut between the two fang holes to draw blood, and then put the stone on the bite area. The stone would stick to the bite area and, although it could take several hours, it would eventually draw the venom out. You'd then have to soak the stone until it was clear, drop it in milk for an hour, wash it and dry it and then it'd be ready to go again. We also always carried a couple of pethidine tablets (an opioid pain reliever) in case of injury, but none of us ever had to use it.

None of us ever needed to try the snake stone, but Jo did say that he had stopped in a village en route to somewhere and came across a young boy who had been bitten by a snake. He applied his stone and they all sat around for at least four hours until the stone came off. He then applied a little bit of bandage to the bite site and left. The boy and certainly all the adults around were very happy with the outcome.

During dinner, Richard said we still had orders to fill for various zoos and parks around the world. It was getting late in the season, so he and Bill and a number of the catchers were going to head back to Uganda to try and get the required animals there. Apart from the gazelle and rhino, Richard felt the capture had been a disaster up here. We all agreed. The terrain for animal capture was terrible and there was an acute shortage of the species we needed. He wanted me to stay there with Geoff to catch more rhino and maybe giant eland, if we could find any.

The following morning, Richard and Bill left and Geoff and I felt we should head back to Shambe to catch the remaining rhino. We thought we'd then go further north and try and find the giant eland there, as they were supposed to be prevalent in the area of Tonj. I gathered my things together and asked Geoff if he was almost ready to set off.

"Oh no, you just carry on and I'll be along shortly," he said.

I wasn't sure what Geoff was up to but ours was not to reason why, we just needed to get on with life, so we set off.

Brian, Masabai and I travelled the seventy-five kilometres down to Juba to cross the Nile, and then headed north. After driving for a good hour or so, we spotted Rory the Pilot obviously en route to Mongalla camp to collect Geoff. Well, now we knew why Geoff had sent us on ahead.

When we travelled, we carried water bags that looked like hessian sack bags. They were almost waterproof, which meant that they leaked and became wet on the outside and as we travelled the air cooled the outside, keeping the water inside cool. Clever, really.

It was late afternoon by the time we arrived at Shambe, and we found the Czechs there, sitting around in camp. I don't think they ever went anywhere or did anything apart from sit around; still, the rhino were for them.

Ann said they were short of meat in camp, so asked if I could bring some in. Brian and I went out with Masabai and, I have to say, although animals seemed to be few and far between there, we managed to find a tiang. We would call this animal a topi, although the Sudan tiang are somewhat larger, and there was plenty of meat on this one, for sure.

Jo thought animals were bigger in the Sudan because of the soil, but I had no idea why they were. Maybe that was why the Dinka were so tall as well. They said it was because of their diet of blood and milk, but I really don't know if that's true.

Chapter 22

The following morning, we were up and ready, awaiting Rory the Pilot's return from his usual morning search for capture candidates. We then ventured out, with Rory guiding us in, but this time we had to travel quite far to find the rhino. I didn't mind though; it was all just another super trip through the bush, very much Africa, but not like Uganda or Kenya.

It is a strange thing to say but the Sudan looked tired, war-fatigued. Areas close to the Nile were better, with more cheery, green vegetation and the swamps, full of elephant and buffalo, were incredible and put something of a gloss on the country for me. But, in general, it was a very sad country, and it was quite difficult to get a smile from its people. I imagine the happiest people in the whole country were the Dinka, who simply kept to themselves and carried on in their own sweet way of life.

We spotted the rhino and, again, the chase was on. Geoff was driving, and it felt like he was aiming for the thickest clumps of acacia to push me through. He wasn't the considerate driver that Richard was, that was for sure. Sometimes Geoff appeared to have quite a sadistic side, like when he injected the guys with penicillin back at Mongalla.

However, we managed to come through it, not completely unscathed, and, as we hit an open spot, I got a rope on the young rhino and we slowed it to a stop. During the capture, we were always totally engrossed in the whole operation, but once the guys had the youngster under control this time, I could feel a trickle of blood running down my neck. It felt like it was nothing serious, in fact just on my neck; my jacket covered most of the rest of me. It was just the odd thorn that had got past my defences and had a ripping time with me; some of the guys also had a little drop of the red juice on their arms and necks too.

Because Richard had taken a number of guys with him to Uganda, we were a little short on manpower on this capture, so I pitched in and helped. When I'd arrived for my first African capture, Charlie had said best to leave the guys to it, as I'd just get in the way. He was right, but now it was different and I think the guys appreciated my help. First, we got the rhino loaded into the crate and then we loaded the crate onto the lorry. It was actually quite fun. The grappling made the muscles work, and in all honesty it was a workout (not that the guys would think so) and it engendered great camaraderie too.

We had another long wait while Rory spotted another one; we laughed and said perhaps we'd already caught all the rhino there were. Rory eventually guided us in to our second catch of the day and this involved another horrendous trip through the acacia bush; even I could see better routes through. Eventually we got the break – a small clearing and then the rhino was caught. Again, once the rhino was controlled, I was off and pitching in to help. The guys always seemed pleased when I did that – we all became part of the same gang – and I enjoyed it too.

Back in camp, we unloaded the two new arrivals. After plenty of snorting and a few mock charges, the rhino eventually backed out of their crate and found shaded sanctuary at the other side of the *boma*. The Czech team seemed happy with the rhino and were all wandering around the *bomas* looking at them too.

It was tea-time again, so Ann and I sat chatting and then Brian joined us too. I told Ann we had to travel up to the Tonj and Wau areas to look for giant eland, and that Geoffrey wanted us to set off early in the morning. After that, I had one of my strip bucket washes in the waters of the White Nile (I make it sound like a boast, but we were fresh out of asses' milk), which was, as always, quite exhilarating and certainly refreshing.

It was then time for dinner, which we all ate together and we all chatted awhile before heading for bed. Geoffrey seemed different, perhaps he was missing our leader or maybe he felt responsible now Richard had gone back to Uganda. Whatever the reason it wasn't good. He seemed quite sullen and distant.

We were up early, with porridge for breakfast, and still no jam. We got our gear together and set off and, for some reason, Geoff wanted us to go directly to Wau, which was beyond Tonj. It didn't really make sense to me, but we headed off anyway. We were quite a convoy: Geoffrey in his vehicle with some of the guys, me driving one with Brian and Masabai, Kiprono, our driver, taking the Bedford truck, Kipsang, the other Kenyan driver taking the Toyota HiAce. and the Czechs following on in their vehicle.

For our first overnight stop, we camped under a flyover of some sort in Wau. I was having trouble with the little finger on my right hand – obviously I had picked up a thorn during the previous day's battle with the acacia. When we were all sitting around a fire, I asked Jo if he had anything he could lance it with, and he produced his pocket knife. He spent ten minutes sharpening it, then sterilising it in the fire. I really wasn't looking forward to what would happen next, but I knew it had to be done; just one blood-curdling scream and it would be all over. His weapon ready, he pulled my hand towards him and, at the moment he was about to strike, I looked away. *Ouuuuch!* I looked at my hand but nothing. Bugger, he'd failed and I'd have to go through that all again. It went in on the third attempt, and then I felt immediate relief. I thanked Jo and was grateful to have no more throbbing pain in my finger, it was now just a little bit sore. I took some of the adhesive tape we used to attach the rope to the catching pole, and wrapped a strip of that around my finger to seal the blister over the wound.

Dinner was a chunk of meat each, with everyone cooking their own on a stick over the fire. I loved it! I had done this a couple of times before and there was just nothing like it. Basically, you'd eat the meat as it cooked by peeling off the cooked outside of the meat and then putting it back over the fire to cook the next layer. It was delicious, albeit heavily salted, as the meat often was after being butchered for hanging and preserving.

There was nothing for us at Wau. It was quite heavily populated, and we needed to be in the bush where the animals were. However, we spent our first night there and all I can say is that I enjoyed my meat. We were wasting our time and should never have gone there, but apparently Geoffrey knew best. The following morning, we moved on to Tonj, having already driven past Tonj to get to Wau.

It was a lot easier to get into the bush at Tonj, but we found it difficult to find a suitable campsite. We found water in each area that looked promising but it was dreadful swamp-water. However, when the Bedford truck broke down, we were forced to make camp in what was far from a good spot. Even after boiling the water for a good ten minutes, it still smelt like swamp. Also, until I could replenish our meat supply, it was maize meal for dinner. The guys liked to eat it thick like mashed potato, which was fine with meat and gravy, but not on its own. Having it like porridge was the best way for me.

The next morning, Geoffrey announced that he and Rory were going to fly to Nairobi to get a new part for the lorry. They took the broken part and then they were gone, leaving us in a difficult situation. I figured I could go out and get meat to keep us going, but I didn't want to go out looking for the giant eland as I could drive all day and find nothing, and all I would have done was waste fuel. Plus, if I found and caught any giant eland, they couldn't live in the capture crates anyway; we needed the lorry to take them to Shambe. All round, it was best to wait for the plane, so that Rory could spot, we could catch, and the lorry could transport the animals.

I went out with Brian and Masabai and shot a tiang, which kept us going for a day or two, but you go through all the meat quickly when fifteen people are tucking in. It took time trying to find game to shoot near camp, and I also felt restricted because the only fuel we had was what we had carried with us, for the vehicles and the plane. If everything went to plan, we would need plenty of fuel for the capture operation, should we find the eland. When we went out for meat, I would see large spoor of what I believed to be eland, but I never saw any.

By the second day, we were all suffering quite badly from diarrhoea, upset stomachs and so on from the water. Two weeks later, we were still sitting and waiting in camp, and our health had not improved. Even the vultures had started gathering and settling in various trees around us when we went bush to the only toilet facility we had. I got the feeling they knew something we didn't.

Each morning, we expected Geoff to return but he didn't, and more and more days went by without any sign of him. I couldn't work out just how long it could take to fly to Nairobi, get a part and fly back. I kept thinking it would only be another day and they would return and we could move on, but no.

After more than two weeks, I was in quite a state health-wise, with something that looked like fungus growing on my face, as well as the ongoing gut problems. The water was contaminated and we couldn't avoid continually taking it in in some form. The local guys seemed to be okay but most of the rest of us were struggling with stomach problems, although the Czechs had a good supply of antiseptics, antibiotics and vitamins.

On one occasion, I went out to shoot something to eat and the only thing I could find was a warthog, which the Czechs were very reluctant to eat for fear of contracting *trichinosis* (a disease you can get from eating raw or under-cooked game meat). On reflection, they were right, but I had it cooked, then minced, and then boiled up again, just to be sure. It was food and we were okay after eating it, so on the third day, they all tucked in too.

I was feeling so unwell, it had become a real chore having to keep going out for meat and, I have to say, on some days I didn't even feel like getting up. It was ridiculous to have to live in such conditions unnecessarily. We couldn't move on and leave the lorry, as it would be unfair to leave one or two guys alone with it as we couldn't ensure their safety.

When I went out with Brian and Masabai one day, I shot three tiang. We most certainly would need it and we had a good supply of salt, if nothing else, and at least we could eat well. One of the animals that I shot was pregnant – not that I could tell – but the Czechs all tucked into the foetus. Well, each to their own.

Having provided meat to keep the camp going, I announced that I would be going back to Shambe. Jo looked at me and nodded and said, "Yes, I think you should."

I don't know why I was so badly affected, maybe it was like eating one bad prawn or mussel, just the luck of the draw. The others were also in far from good health, but I felt I needed to get away from this camp.

The next day, Brian, Masabai and I drove back to Shambe, where immediately the water was better – that wonderful, boiled-for-ten-minutes Nile water. What a relief! The food was better too, although I needed to get some meat in for the camp there as well. When I told Ann the tale of what had happened at Tonj, she nodded and said she wasn't surprised.

"He still isn't back?" she said.

"No, still not back, and it's been more than two weeks now," I said.

We stayed at Shambe the next day, and then the three of us set out for Mongalla. It was a fun trip, but when we arrived at the long bridge made from wooden poles, a lorry had dropped a back wheel through it. The driver had kept to the centre of the bridge and had got stuck halfway along it, completely blocking the bridge. By the time we got there, there was a gang of people coming towards us armed with poles, and they set about lifting the lorry out of the bridge. We all got out to help too as we were stuck until the lorry was out. I have to say, I didn't think it was possible but, with the aid of the poles and everyone pushing and lifting, the lorry came out and moved off over the bridge. At the end of the bridge, which was about a hundred and fifty yards long, the driver stopped and made some sort of settlement with the gang.

Brian and Masabai then watched as I slowly spanned the hole that the lorry had left, then all aboard and we were on our way again. It was certainly hot and dusty and we were pleased we had our two water sacks, giving us cool water. When we reached Juba, I headed for the Juba Hotel, where we all sat and drank the cold but dubious orange juice, two large glasses each.

Then we continued on to camp. When we reached Mongalla village, there was a paddle steamer in, so after checking in with the police, we simply sat and watched the hurly-burly of a day in the life of folk in the village. To me, it was all fun and amusement, fascination, but no doubt to the locals it was quite a chore, a painstaking method of eking out a living.

It was a relief to arrive in Mongalla camp, and to be able to just chill out. It had been a long trip, with many toilet stops along the way. Brian was suffering too but I was feeling quite weak and I'm sure dehydrated as I had been limiting the intake of what I considered diseased water. I'd had almost three weeks of this now, and I decided I needed to fly to Nairobi to get some medical treatment. Ann said she thought she would come and see us off at the airport. Ann and I were quite close really, and we seemed to understand each other well.

After a good night's sleep, I managed to have some of Zapiel's bread in the morning and then Brian, Ann and I set out for Juba Airport in the hopes of finding Brian and me a flight to Nairobi. At the airport, I had a little argy-bargy with immigration as I had overstayed my visa. After handing him enough money to buy his wife a new coat, the problem was miraculously solved.

Ann went off to speak to some people and, on her return, said there was a plane owned by Dutch people who were building a bridge in Juba, and they had a spare seat to Nairobi. They were due to leave in around an hour. I was soon to be on my way. Brian managed to get a seat on a scheduled flight later in the day, so we were all set. I thanked Ann for getting me organised and finding me a flight and I was soon gone.

I felt quite ill during the flight down to Wilson Airport in Nairobi and was very relieved to arrive there. I took a taxi to the Hilton Hotel, and asked at the desk if Geoffrey Gibbon was staying there. They rang his room for me, and he told me to hang on in reception and he would come down.

I was then very surprised to see Richard, his lady friend, and Gibbon, all walking through the lobby towards me. The Hilton Hotel in Nairobi was quite a contrast in living standards to our swamp in the Sudanese bush, and I wondered how much longer the others would have to remain there before Gibbon eventually made it back. I knew for a fact I could have had a part for the Bedford lorry flown out from England to Nairobi within three days, so why they would wait all this time in Nairobi for one, I had no idea.

Brian then arrived and asked if I had a hotel room, which I didn't yet. He told me to go with him to stay at the Thorntree Hotel around the corner.

"My grandmother told me I should stay there given the chance, and this is it," Brian said. "It is actually called the New Stanley Hotel, but there's a very large thorn tree growing outside, which I believe was the original name. Don't worry about the cost, I will pay for it – my treat."

I had to get my agenda organised for the next day. Apart from everything else, I'd had toothache for quite a while, so I needed to see a dentist as well as a doctor. I took the first free appointments they could give me, and once they were booked, Brian and I went round to the Thorntree. I actually knew it quite well and I was happy to show Brian the Long Bar, where my friend Mike said more elephants had been shot than in the whole of Africa. We had a drink there and another under the thorn tree outside, and it was good to be able to get a couple of Tusker beers down.

Brian managed to arrange his flight back to the States the following evening. I said my farewells to him the next morning over breakfast, as I had no idea how my day would pan out. First, the dentist, who gave me a temporary filling, and then on to see a doctor, who took the odd sample from me and told me to come back and see him the following day. When I got there the next morning, it wasn't good news: he recommended I go into hospital for more tests and told me to expect to be there for at least two weeks. With me likely to need treatment after that, I could be in hospital for many weeks.

The obvious solution, from my point of view, was to return home to England and get my treatment there. After talking it through with Richard, he agreed and organised a flight for me. The earliest booking they could get me on was a Sudanese flight, but at least I would be home by the morning.

Sudan Airways was not an airline I would recommend anyone fly with, I'm afraid. We flew from Nairobi to Khartoum, where we passengers stood on the runway for four hours while they found a plane for us. During that time, I made many safaris to find the toilet and, once we were in the air, the in-flight service was all but non-existent. I consoled myself by taking the attitude that it was only time and all would be well, which of course it was.

We got into London Heathrow the following morning around 8am, which was a bit later than scheduled. Mike met me at the arrival hall, and it was good to see him on his feet after his accident in Karamoja. Mike and I had known each other for some years, and I was quick to tell him we'd been drinking in the Long Bar the day before.

Mike dropped me at the door of my mother's house, which was in fact opposite the doctor's surgery. My mother was very surprised to see me, as she had no idea I was coming, so after greeting her I went over to see the doctor. He made arrangements for me to be admitted to the Tropical Disease Hospital in London that evening.

In hospital, I had treatments and a huge number of tests for a range of diseases I'd never even heard of. Being back in a hygienic environment was a great start to my healing, but no-one seemed to know what the fungus was that was growing on my face. It did start to heal after a few weeks and the dysentery they said I had soon became far more manageable too.

When the sister arrived at my hospital bed in the mornings, she'd often say, "Good morning, Mr Litchfield. Ready? Torture chamber for you today."

She'd then lead me off to have various chrome instruments, cables and wires inserted into every bodily cavity and orifice I had.

After a couple of weeks, they let me out at weekends if I wasn't having a specific treatment. When I was on one of my weekend breaks, the good old malaria struck, reducing me to a quivering wreck for around twelve hours. On reflection, I had probably stopped taking my quinine tablets too soon and I had no doubt also contracted malaria, as I had the other ailments, during our spell in the swamps.

I began to feel normal but, on the second day, whack, it hit again. I'd contracted the forty-eight-hour-cycle malaria and so I had periods of feeling not too bad before reverting to a shaking heap. After a week, they seemed to get it under control with various quinines.

I was also diagnosed with *giardia lamblia* (a stomach bug caused by a tiny parasite), again no doubt contracted in the swamp from contaminated food and or water.

I remained in hospital for a total of three months, and I was eventually discharged but it took around eighteen months for me to return to something like normal health again. It was only after some specialist treatment for *schistosomiasis* (originally known as bilharzia, which I'd been tested and treated for when I first went into hospital), which a doctor at the London School of Tropical Medicine prescribed for me some fifteen years later, that my health really started to improve.

Meanwhile, back in Africa, I don't know how long it was before Geoff returned to Tonj with the lorry part or how long they all waited for him – I never got news from there. Jo did some rhino counting in the Shambe area, with Rory flying him around, and when the Czechs and Terry left, it was just Ann, Geoffrey and Bruce, who was sent out to construct the crates for the rhino, who were left there.

Life had become very difficult with the authorities, I understand, so they decided to get the rhino out and into Uganda, which they succeeded in doing. They released the gazelles back into the area where we'd caught them, and then they left; Geoffrey travelled with the lorry, Bruce drove another truck, and Ann took a Humber truck with a small rhino on board.

The authorities gave Ann a very hard time and refused to give her an exit visa, as her visa had expired (like mine had). As a young blonde female, she knew very well what the officials wanted before they'd rectify the situation, so she faked an engine problem on the last hill. She waited until the other two vehicles had cleared no-man's-land, and then turned again and charged through the barrier to the Ugandan border. Ann was a strong individual and very capable, she would have done this without giving it a second thought!

They all then headed out to Karamoja, where Richard had set up camp for giraffe and antelope capture, just north of Chepsikunya, alongside Greek River. There, they prepared to get the rhino – along with the giraffe and antelope Richard had caught – transported out of the country.

Richard was in camp when they arrived, but left a couple of days later for Chambura, where he'd been capturing elephant. It was on that return trip to Chambura from Karamoja, on the 18th of April 1975, that a fatal road accident took Richard's life and left Bill with a life-changing injury.

I found the news of Richard's death quite shocking. I'd spent a great deal of time in his company as we'd travelled together for months at a time, often working eighteen-hour days together. He was my boss, the Boss, but he was my friend too. Despite our telepathic connection, neither of us saw that coming. His death changed many lives and no doubt the situation will have been very traumatic for everyone else too.

As I understand it, Jo did manage to catch a few giraffe to make up the shortfall in his orders. Mike and another colleague were drafted in to Uganda to help wind things up and get the animals out and, once all the animals were shipped out, Ann was the last to leave. She travelled with the rhino by road to Tororo, then by train to Mombasa, where she waited with them until a ship was available to transport them to a port where the Czechs would meet them and take them to their new home. Unbelievably, after all that, the Czech team didn't send a keeper to travel back with the valuable rhino cargo, so the ship's crew took care of them.

We'd also been due to capture an eighth rhino, which would have given a pair to the Khartoum Zoo, but they just got the one as, after I left, it just didn't happen.

Chapter 23

The sudden unexpected transportation of this village kid, in January 1974, into the wider world was life-changing, a little scary but mostly fascinating and educational. My focus had changed from the everyday to a much wider vision of life outside of village life. I don't knock village life, I was a very happy person before travelling further afield and happiness is extremely important wherever and whatever you do. In truth, I will always be a village kid. However, I am a great believer in fate – some may say luck – and my travels had not just been new but very exciting and a huge amount of fun.

Our capture work was extremely hazardous work and we carried it out in volatile, often hostile countries. I am proud to have been part of the team that went into those countries to capture and preserve such endangered species, in particular the northern white rhino, *Ceratotherium simum cottoni*. The animals we caught always had the best of food and care, our local staff and camp managers were excellent, and their work was of a very high standard. No-one would prosper from a dead or injured animal. Richard ran an extremely professional, caring business; he gave his best and he expected the best from his staff too.

Richard's death changed many a life direction, however, it was his life that was most life-changing for me. I have never been a follower (I'm far too self-centred for that) but Richard definitely became my mentor throughout that magical, African period of my life.

From Richard, I learned self-respect; I learned that people in authority can be nice people, I learned the value of leading by example, through ability and hard work, and I learned that focus is the key. "Take care of staff," he would say with a chuckle, "or otherwise you will have a hell of a lot of work to do yourself."

Africa taught me that happiness and contentment can be very simple. I met people who had very little (by western standards anyway) but who had absolutely everything they required, in reality making them happy, jolly people and a pleasure to be around.

The African guys that I worked with were people of the land and at one with the land: from trackers and hunters to fishermen, each appeared to own a small amount of *shamba* (land) where they would grow food, keep chickens and maybe the odd goat for meat and eggs, making them quite self-sufficient.

As for my work, once I was cleared by the hospital, I returned to Woburn Safari Park, eventually taking charge as Curator in 1978. I remained there until 1986, when I went to Thailand for the building of Bangkok Safari World.

Woburn had always been my home and life was good. I enjoyed my work, living in a community that I had grown up in and having family all around me too.

As we travel through life, we collect material items – a present, a useful tool, binoculars, a knife, and so on. We also collect memories, experiences (both good and bad) and, when all is added together, they make people what they are or what they will become.

Africa did that for me. It helped shape the person I am today. When I speak of Africa, it is East Africa that is most familiar to me. The fond memories I have of those countries, the adventures and experiences we had there, and the people and animals that made such an impression on me while I was there, have all made me who I am and will always be a part of me.

KAMATA KAMATA KAMATA

172

Northern White Rhino Sudan soon after his capture 1975

Brian Vidor

Shambe Rhino Camp

Convoy arrival in Sudan

Capture of the rhino, Rhino Sudan

Camp at the side of the road

Me with some of the gang

Me with Masabai, photo by Brian Vidor

Making biltong with Masabai

Wildman of the Sudan